Tech Wealth

Building Financial Freedom in the Digital Age

By Oluchi Ike

Preface

In today's fast-paced world, technology has changed every aspect of our lives, including how we build, manage, and grow wealth. Traditional wealth-building methods, while still valuable, often feel limited in a landscape that now includes digital currencies, AI-driven investment platforms, and global freelance opportunities. **Tech Wealth: Building Financial Freedom in the Digital Age** is designed to guide you through the vast world of technology-driven wealth-building tools and strategies, making it accessible and actionable.

Whether you're a young professional, an entrepreneur, or someone simply curious about tech's role in financial freedom, this book provides the roadmap you need. We'll explore the digital economy, from remote work and e-commerce to emerging trends like cryptocurrency and blockchain. Along the way, you'll discover tools, strategies, and stories of people who've built wealth through innovation and a willingness to embrace new technology.

The goal of this book is to help you understand how technology can empower your financial journey and equip you with practical steps to achieve financial independence. From leveraging online platforms for income to automating your investments, every chapter is crafted to inspire and guide you on your journey to tech-driven wealth.

Welcome to the future of finance. Let's start building your **Tech Wealth**.

Table of Contents

Preface

Part 1: Introduction to Tech Wealth-Building

1. **The Digital Age of Wealth-Building**

    - Overview of the shift from traditional to tech-based financial growth

    - Why tech is essential for modern wealth strategies

    - Common myths and misconceptions about tech-based wealth-building

---

Part 2: Income Streams in the Digital World

2. **The Rise of Remote Work and Freelance Opportunities**

    - Platforms to kickstart your remote work journey

    - Building a portfolio and maximizing freelance income

    - Strategies for budgeting and saving in a fluctuating income environment

3. **Creating Digital Income: E-commerce, Dropshipping, and Online Services**

    - Starting an online store: choosing products, platforms, and marketing

    - Dropshipping, print-on-demand, and service-based businesses

    - How to build passive income with digital products

Part 3: Digital Investment Essentials

4. **Cryptocurrency and Blockchain for Beginners**

    - Understanding crypto basics, blockchain technology, and wallets

- Investing in cryptocurrencies: risks, rewards, and popular platforms
- NFTs and other blockchain assets as wealth-building tools

5. **Automating Wealth: AI and Financial Automation Tools**
    - The power of robo-advisors and automated investing
    - AI-driven savings apps and digital financial advisors
    - Balancing automation with personalized financial management

6. **Navigating the Fintech World: Apps and Platforms for Financial Growth**
    - Overview of top fintech tools for investment, budgeting, and saving
    - Peer-to-peer lending, crowdfunding, and micro-investing
    - Choosing the best fintech solutions for your financial goals

---

Part 4: Leveraging Knowledge and Skills for Wealth

7. **Upskilling for Profit: The Power of Online Education**
    - High-demand skills in the tech and digital space
    - Best platforms for online learning and certification
    - Using your new skills to negotiate higher pay or start a side business

8. **Monetizing Content Creation: Social Media, Blogging, and Streaming**
    - Strategies for building and monetizing a personal brand
    - Social media income streams: affiliate marketing, ads, and sponsorships

- Tips for successful content creation on platforms like YouTube and TikTok

---

Part 5: Real and Virtual Assets

9. **Digital Real Estate: Crowdfunding and Virtual Property Investment**

    - Introduction to real estate crowdfunding and REITs
    - Investing in virtual properties in the metaverse
    - Pros and cons of traditional vs. digital real estate investments

10. **Exploring Stock Market Options Through Tech**

    - Overview of stock trading apps and online brokerages
    - Understanding ETFs, fractional shares, and index funds
    - How to analyze stocks with tech tools for smarter investing

---

Part 6: Protecting and Growing Your Wealth

11. **Cybersecurity for Your Digital Wealth**

    - Securing your online investments and protecting your assets
    - Common scams to watch out for and how to avoid them
    - Best practices for online privacy and financial security

12. **Future Trends and Technologies Impacting Wealth**

    - Exploring future tech innovations like IoT, AI, and 5G

- Emerging financial opportunities in new tech sectors
- How to stay updated and prepare for future shifts in wealth-building

Part 7: Building Your Tech Wealth Plan

13. **Creating Your Personalized Tech Wealth-Building Strategy**
    - Setting clear financial goals for your tech wealth journey
    - Building a sustainable plan with diverse income and investment sources
    - Practical steps for integrating tech tools into your daily financial routine

14. **Balancing Traditional and Tech-Driven Approaches to Wealth**
    - Combining traditional investments with tech opportunities
    - Creating a well-rounded, resilient portfolio
    - Keeping a long-term mindset in a fast-evolving financial landscape

Appendices

- **Glossary of Key Terms**
- **Resources and Recommended Tools**
- **Further Reading and Suggested Courses**
- **Index**

This structure provides a clear and practical roadmap for readers, with actionable insights and diverse tech-driven wealth-building options. Let me know if you'd like to adjust or add anything!

Part 1: Introduction to Tech Wealth-Building

Chapter 1: The Digital Age of Wealth-Building

1.1 Overview of the Shift from Traditional to Tech-Based Financial Growth

In recent decades, technology has reshaped the financial landscape, creating pathways to wealth that were unimaginable just a generation ago. Traditional wealth-building methods—such as investing in stocks, real estate, and retirement accounts—remain valuable, but they often require large capital, patience, and a high degree of financial literacy. The rise of digital tools, however, has lowered these barriers, enabling anyone with an internet connection to access opportunities for income generation, investing, and even asset creation.

From robo-advisors that automate investments to online marketplaces where people can start businesses with minimal capital, technology has democratized access to wealth-building strategies. Cryptocurrency and blockchain technology offer entirely new asset classes, while the gig economy and remote work allow people to earn money beyond traditional employment models. This shift has not only broadened the scope of wealth-building opportunities but has also accelerated the pace at which individuals can grow their finances. For those willing to learn, adapt, and take calculated risks, technology offers unparalleled potential to achieve financial freedom.

1.2 Why Tech is Essential for Modern Wealth Strategies

Technology has become an essential component of modern wealth strategies for several reasons. Firstly, technology enables accessibility. Fintech apps, online investment platforms, and digital payment systems make it easy for people to participate in the financial world regardless of location or background. A person in a small town can invest in international markets or run an online business, expanding their opportunities without needing to relocate or have direct access to traditional financial institutions.

Secondly, technology drives efficiency. Automated investment platforms and AI-powered financial tools reduce the need for hands-on management, freeing up time for individuals to focus on other wealth-building activities or to simply enjoy life. Technology also enables smarter decision-making. Financial analysis tools and data-driven insights give users the ability to make informed decisions, minimizing risk and maximizing returns.

Thirdly, technology offers diversification. Digital assets, remote work, e-commerce, content creation, and crowdfunding all represent unique income streams. By diversifying across these tech-driven avenues, individuals can build a resilient financial portfolio. Technology isn't just a tool; it is a foundation upon which new, diversified, and agile wealth strategies can be built.

1.3 Common Myths and Misconceptions About Tech-Based Wealth-Building

While technology provides many benefits for wealth-building, several myths and misconceptions can deter people from taking advantage of these opportunities. Understanding these misconceptions is crucial for embracing the full potential of tech-driven financial growth.

- **Myth #1: Tech Wealth-Building is Only for the Young or Tech-Savvy.** Many assume that to thrive financially with technology, one must be highly skilled in tech or a part of the younger generation. This belief is unfounded. While younger people may be more accustomed to technology, the tools available today are designed for ease of use, making them accessible to users of all ages and skill levels. Robo-advisors, for example, simplify the investing process for beginners, while e-commerce platforms provide step-by-step guidance to help users launch online stores without prior experience.

- **Myth #2: Investing in Digital Assets is Too Risky.**
  While it's true that some digital assets like cryptocurrencies are volatile, not all tech-based wealth-building strategies carry extreme risks. Robo-advisors, for instance, use algorithms to manage diversified portfolios, often making them less risky than single-stock investments. Understanding the range of options and risk levels is essential to make informed choices rather than avoiding tech-driven investments altogether.

- **Myth #3: Only Large Investments Yield Significant Returns in Tech.**
  Unlike traditional wealth-building, tech-based growth often allows people to start with small amounts of money. Many digital platforms offer micro-investing, where even $5 or $10 can be invested in fractional shares or peer-to-peer lending options. Additionally, freelancing, content creation, and e-commerce don't require substantial startup capital but can generate considerable returns over time. With the right approach, small investments can yield meaningful returns in the digital landscape.

By dispelling these myths, we can start seeing tech wealth-building for what it is: an inclusive, diverse, and flexible means of financial growth that's accessible to nearly everyone.

Key Takeaways

- Technology has significantly broadened access to wealth-building opportunities, making it easier for anyone with an internet connection to participate.

- Tech is essential for modern wealth strategies due to its accessibility, efficiency, and potential for diversification.

- Common myths, such as tech-based wealth-building being exclusive to young or highly tech-savvy individuals, can discourage people from exploring these valuable opportunities.

This chapter serves as a foundational understanding of why technology is a game-changer for wealth-building and addresses common misconceptions that often hold people back from capitalizing on these innovations.

Part 2: Income Streams in the Digital World

Chapter 2: The Rise of Remote Work and Freelance Opportunities

The rapid digital transformation has opened doors for people to work remotely and freelance, creating a shift in how individuals think about employment, income, and lifestyle. Remote work and freelancing offer flexibility, autonomy, and a wide range of opportunities for people across the globe. These alternative work styles are attractive not only for their convenience but also for their ability to empower people to choose projects that align with their skills and passions. This chapter explores the foundations of remote work and freelancing, from the best platforms to start with, to building a portfolio, and financial strategies for managing the fluctuating income that comes with freelancing.

2.1 Platforms to Kickstart Your Remote Work Journey

For anyone looking to start working remotely, a wide array of platforms makes the transition easier and provides opportunities to connect with clients, secure projects, and build a reputation. The following are some of the most popular platforms where new and seasoned freelancers alike can kickstart their journey:

- **Upwork:** One of the largest and most versatile platforms, Upwork offers opportunities across a wide range of industries including writing, programming, marketing, and design. Freelancers can create a profile, list their skills, and bid on projects that interest them. Upwork uses a rating system, so building a solid reputation over time can lead to better-paying opportunities.

- **Fiverr:** Known for its "gig-based" structure, Fiverr allows freelancers to post specific services they offer at various price points. Clients browse these gigs and can directly hire freelancers based on the offered packages. This platform is particularly useful for creative professionals like graphic designers, voice actors, and social media managers.

- **LinkedIn:** While primarily a social networking site for professionals, LinkedIn is also a powerful tool for finding remote work opportunities. Many companies and clients post jobs or search for freelancers through LinkedIn, and connecting directly with potential clients can often lead to remote work or freelance gigs.

- **Freelancer.com:** Another popular platform, Freelancer.com allows freelancers to bid on projects in various fields, from data entry to software development. The platform hosts contests, allowing freelancers to showcase their work, gain visibility, and potentially secure new clients.

- **Remote.co and We Work Remotely:** These are job boards dedicated to remote work, listing both freelance and full-time remote positions across sectors. Remote.co focuses on remote-friendly companies and often lists more traditional positions, while We Work Remotely caters to freelancers and remote job seekers in tech, design, and other fields.

For those beginning their remote work journey, it's important to test several platforms, explore their unique structures, and find which ones align best with their skills and goals. Each platform has its own fee structures and payout policies, so understanding these details helps maximize earnings.

2.2 Building a Portfolio and Maximizing Freelance Income

In freelancing, a strong portfolio is essential for attracting clients and standing out in a competitive market. A portfolio showcases your skills, past projects, and demonstrates to potential clients the value you can offer. Here are steps to build a compelling portfolio and strategies for maximizing freelance income:

- **Creating a Focused Portfolio:** Start by selecting samples of your work that highlight your core skills and strengths. If you're a writer, choose samples that showcase your versatility and quality, while designers might include a mix of styles. Make sure your portfolio is tailored to your target audience and emphasizes the types of work you're most interested in attracting. Even if you're new to freelancing, consider creating mock projects or offering services to friends or small businesses to build up a collection of sample work.

- **Using Case Studies to Demonstrate Impact:** For each sample, consider including a brief description of the project, the challenges involved, and how your work contributed to the client's success. Quantifying your impact—such as showing how a website redesign increased a client's conversions—can significantly improve your portfolio's effectiveness.

- **Networking and Building Client Relationships:** Positive client relationships are essential in freelancing. Satisfied clients are likely to offer repeat work and may even recommend you to others. Be proactive in communication, ask questions, and deliver high-quality work to create lasting client relationships. Networking through professional groups or communities, whether in-person or online, can also lead to new opportunities and collaborations.

- **Upselling and Offering Additional Services:** If you notice a client has ongoing needs that align with your skills, consider offering additional services. For instance, a writer could suggest a content calendar, or a designer might offer ongoing brand updates. Upselling relevant services adds value for the client while increasing your income without having to seek out new clients constantly.

- **Specializing in a Niche Market:** Specialization can make you more attractive to certain clients and allow you to command higher rates. For instance, a web developer who specializes in e-commerce sites or a copywriter who focuses on tech companies will likely find it easier to attract high-paying clients within those niches.

By building a portfolio that showcases quality, relevance, and impact, freelancers can position themselves to command higher rates, secure long-term clients, and maximize their income potential.

2.3 Strategies for Budgeting and Saving in a Fluctuating Income Environment

One of the biggest challenges in freelancing is managing a fluctuating income. Unlike traditional employment with a steady paycheck, freelancers often experience varying income from month to month, which requires careful budgeting and financial planning. Here are effective strategies to manage finances as a freelancer:

- **Creating an Emergency Fund:** Building and maintaining an emergency fund is essential for freelancers. Aim to save three to six months' worth of living expenses to cover periods when work may be slower or unexpected expenses arise. An emergency fund provides peace of mind and financial security in uncertain times.

- **Setting Aside Taxes:** Since freelance income typically doesn't have taxes withheld, it's important to set aside a percentage of each payment for taxes. Many freelancers set aside 25-30% of each payment to cover income and self-employment taxes. Creating a separate savings account for taxes can help keep these funds distinct and avoid surprises during tax season.

- **Using Budgeting Tools:** Digital budgeting tools like Mint, YNAB (You Need a Budget), or QuickBooks Self-Employed help freelancers track income, categorize expenses, and maintain a clear picture of their financial health. Budgeting tools are especially helpful for freelancers to manage variable income, track overdue invoices, and project monthly expenses.

- **Establishing Consistent Invoicing Practices:** Getting paid on time is crucial for financial stability. Use a consistent invoicing system and agree on payment terms with clients before starting any work. Tools like FreshBooks, Wave, or PayPal Invoicing offer templates and automated reminders to help freelancers keep track of payments.

- **Living Below Your Means During High-Income Periods:** Freelancers often experience high-earning months followed by slower periods. During months with a higher income, avoid the temptation to increase spending. Instead, save a portion of the excess income to cushion leaner months, building a "financial buffer" for your freelance business.

- **Automating Savings and Investments:** Even with fluctuating income, consistent saving is possible. Many freelancers set up automatic transfers to savings accounts or investment portfolios based on a percentage of their monthly income. Automating savings ensures that a portion of income is regularly set aside, helping build wealth over time.

Freelancers who adopt smart budgeting and saving practices are better prepared to handle the ups and downs of freelance income. By planning ahead and setting financial goals, freelancers can achieve a level of stability that ensures their freelance career supports their lifestyle without creating financial stress.

Key Takeaways

- Multiple platforms offer freelancers opportunities to start their remote work journey, each with unique advantages for various industries.

- Building a portfolio and nurturing client relationships are essential to maximizing freelance income.
- Freelancers must adopt financial planning strategies, including budgeting, saving, and creating an emergency fund, to handle the irregular nature of freelance income.

This chapter provides a roadmap for freelancers to navigate their careers effectively, build sustainable income streams, and develop a resilient financial plan that supports long-term goals. With the right tools, strategies, and mindset, freelancing can offer not just flexibility but also significant financial rewards.

Part 2: Income Streams in the Digital World

Chapter 3: Creating Digital Income: E-commerce, Dropshipping, and Online Services

As the world shifts increasingly online, so do opportunities for creating income streams. E-commerce, dropshipping, and online services represent some of the most lucrative avenues for digital entrepreneurs. Whether you're looking to build a side hustle, achieve financial freedom, or transition to a digital-first career, creating a digital income stream can be a game-changer. This chapter delves into the fundamentals of establishing a digital business, from choosing products and platforms for an online store, to understanding the logistics of dropshipping and print-on-demand, to harnessing the potential of digital products for passive income.

3.1 Starting an Online Store: Choosing Products, Platforms, and Marketing

Creating an online store is one of the most popular ways to generate income in today's digital landscape. With platforms and tools available to help anyone set up shop, it's an appealing option, but building a successful online store requires strategic decisions in product selection, platform choice, and marketing.

- **Choosing the Right Products**: The foundation of any successful online store is the products offered. Choosing the right products involves researching market demand, competition, and target audience. Start by considering the following:

    - **Passion and Expertise**: Selling products you're passionate about or knowledgeable in can be a competitive advantage. If you understand the target audience well, it's easier to position your store to meet their needs.

    - **Market Demand**: Tools like Google Trends, Amazon Best Sellers, and social media can help identify products currently in demand. Focus on products with consistent interest rather than short-lived trends.

- **Profit Margins**: Consider the cost of production, shipping, and marketing when selecting products. Low-margin products may require higher sales volumes to be profitable, while high-margin products may have a slower sales rate but better profitability.

- **Choosing the Right Platform**: Once you've chosen products, selecting the right e-commerce platform is essential. Popular platforms include:
    - **Shopify**: Known for its ease of use and extensive integrations, Shopify is one of the most popular choices for e-commerce. It allows you to customize your store, manage products, and handle payment processing seamlessly.
    - **WooCommerce**: A plugin for WordPress, WooCommerce is a good option for those familiar with WordPress who want more control over their store. It offers flexibility but may require more technical setup.
    - **Amazon or Etsy**: If you prefer to tap into an existing customer base, platforms like Amazon and Etsy are great options. They provide exposure to millions of buyers, though they also have higher fees and some limitations on branding and customization.
    - **BigCommerce**: Similar to Shopify, BigCommerce is another comprehensive platform that provides robust e-commerce features with scalability for larger businesses.

- **Marketing Your Store**: Effective marketing is key to driving traffic and generating sales. Here are some proven strategies:

- **Social Media Marketing**: Platforms like Instagram, Facebook, and TikTok are powerful channels for reaching a broad audience. Visual content and influencer partnerships can be especially effective.

- **Search Engine Optimization (SEO)**: Optimizing your product listings and website for search engines can help you rank higher on search results, driving organic traffic over time.

- **Email Marketing**: Building an email list allows you to nurture potential customers and promote new products or sales directly. Offering a discount or freebie in exchange for an email signup is a common tactic.

- **Paid Ads**: Running targeted ads on Google, Facebook, or Instagram can be a fast way to drive traffic, though it requires a budget and careful tracking of return on investment (ROI).

By carefully selecting products, platforms, and marketing strategies, you can create a solid foundation for a successful online store that generates steady income.

3.2 Dropshipping, Print-on-Demand, and Service-Based Businesses

While traditional e-commerce requires managing inventory, dropshipping, print-on-demand, and service-based businesses offer ways to operate without the need for large upfront investments or product storage. Each model has its own unique characteristics and benefits.

- **Dropshipping**: This model allows you to sell products without holding inventory. When a customer places an order, the supplier ships the product directly to the buyer. Dropshipping is attractive because it has lower startup costs and less risk, though it's crucial to work with reliable suppliers to ensure product quality and delivery times.

- **Finding Suppliers**: Platforms like AliExpress, Oberlo (integrated with Shopify), and Spocket connect dropshippers with suppliers worldwide. Researching supplier reviews and ordering samples is recommended to assess product quality.

- **Marketing**: Since dropshipping has thin margins, effective marketing is critical. Successful dropshippers often focus on niche markets and use paid ads to drive targeted traffic.

- **Print-on-Demand (POD)**: Print-on-demand businesses allow you to design products (like T-shirts, mugs, or posters) that are only printed once a customer places an order. POD is popular among artists, designers, and entrepreneurs who want to create custom products without upfront inventory.

  - **Choosing a POD Platform**: Popular POD platforms include Printful, Printify, and Teespring. Many of these services integrate with e-commerce platforms, simplifying the selling process.

  - **Designing Products**: Creativity and trend awareness are essential in POD. Consider seasonal or niche designs that resonate with specific audiences. Testing multiple designs and monitoring sales data helps identify top-performing products.

- **Service-Based Businesses**: If you possess specific skills like graphic design, copywriting, or digital marketing, offering services online can be a straightforward way to earn income.

- **Setting Up**: Create a professional portfolio and list your services on platforms like Fiverr, Upwork, or LinkedIn. Alternatively, building a personal website provides credibility and a way to showcase your work.

- **Maximizing Income**: Service-based businesses can be scaled by offering packages, upselling, or adding retainer options for ongoing clients. Over time, building a reputation through positive reviews and referrals can lead to more clients and higher rates.

These models enable flexibility and minimal overhead, making them accessible ways to build digital income streams that suit different skill sets and levels of experience.

3.3 How to Build Passive Income with Digital Products

One of the most attractive aspects of digital income streams is the potential for passive income, where you can earn money with minimal ongoing effort. Digital products, such as e-books, online courses, and templates, offer substantial passive income potential and scalability.

- **Identifying Profitable Digital Products**: Start by identifying what knowledge, skills, or resources you can transform into a digital product. Popular types of digital products include:

  - **E-books**: E-books on niche topics are popular among those looking to gain knowledge quickly. Platforms like Amazon Kindle Direct Publishing (KDP) make it easy to publish and reach a global audience.

- **Online Courses**: If you have expertise in a specific area, creating an online course can be highly lucrative. Platforms like Udemy, Teachable, and Skillshare provide easy-to-use tools for course creation and promotion.

- **Templates and Digital Assets**: Templates for business, design, or productivity (such as resume templates, social media graphics, or Excel spreadsheets) sell well on platforms like Etsy or Gumroad. They're easy to create once and can be sold repeatedly with minimal upkeep.

- **Marketing Digital Products**: Effective marketing is crucial to building awareness and driving sales for digital products. Strategies include:

  - **Building an Email List**: Offering a free sample or mini-course can encourage visitors to subscribe to your email list. You can then promote your digital products directly to your list, maximizing conversions.

  - **Using Content Marketing**: Blogging, YouTube, and social media content can help establish your expertise and attract traffic to your products. By creating valuable content related to your digital products, you build trust and interest among potential buyers.

  - **Leveraging Affiliate Marketing**: Partnering with affiliates who can promote your products on their channels can increase reach and sales. Offer affiliates a commission for each sale they drive, motivating them to promote your product to their audience.

- **Automating Sales and Delivery**: One of the benefits of digital products is the ability to automate sales and distribution. Platforms like Shopify,

Gumroad, and SendOwl allow for automatic delivery upon purchase, eliminating the need for hands-on fulfillment.

Building passive income with digital products requires upfront effort in creating and marketing but can yield long-term benefits and financial stability. With the right strategies and a commitment to quality, digital products offer the potential for sustainable income.

Key Takeaways

- Building an online store requires strategic choices in products, platforms, and marketing to establish a sustainable business.

- Dropshipping, print-on-demand, and service-based businesses offer flexible, low-cost options for creating digital income streams without inventory.

- Passive income from digital products like e-books, online courses, and templates offers scalability and long-term earning potential with minimal upkeep.

This chapter provides a guide to creating diverse digital income streams, helping readers leverage modern tools and platforms to unlock financial opportunities. By focusing on strategy, quality, and effective marketing, individuals can turn their digital ventures into sustainable income sources.

Part 3: Digital Investment Essentials

Chapter 4: Cryptocurrency and Blockchain for Beginners

The rise of cryptocurrency and blockchain technology has revolutionized the financial world, providing new and diverse ways to invest, build wealth, and diversify portfolios. However, for beginners, the terminology and volatility of crypto assets can be intimidating. This chapter will guide you through the essentials of cryptocurrency, from understanding the basics of blockchain technology and crypto wallets to exploring the opportunities and risks of investing in cryptocurrencies and blockchain assets like NFTs. As with any financial endeavor, knowledge is power, so let's dive into the world of digital assets.

4.1 Understanding Crypto Basics, Blockchain Technology, and Wallets

What is Cryptocurrency?

Cryptocurrency is a form of digital currency designed to work as a medium of exchange through a decentralized technology called blockchain. Unlike traditional currencies issued by governments, cryptocurrencies are maintained by a distributed network of computers, enhancing security and transparency. Cryptocurrencies like Bitcoin, Ethereum, and Litecoin can be used for various transactions and have become increasingly popular as investment assets.

Blockchain Technology Explained

Blockchain is the backbone of cryptocurrency. It's a decentralized digital ledger that records transactions across a network of computers, making the data nearly impossible to alter retroactively. Here's how it works:

1. **Blocks**: Each "block" contains a group of transactions. Once a block is filled, it is linked to the previous block, creating a "chain" of blocks.

2. **Decentralization**: Unlike a traditional database controlled by a single authority, a blockchain is maintained by a network of computers, or "nodes," which work together to validate and record transactions.

3. **Security and Transparency**: Since transactions are stored across multiple nodes and encrypted, blockchain is highly secure. It's also transparent—anyone with access can view the blockchain, although specific details of each transaction remain anonymous.

This decentralized structure makes blockchain ideal for secure transactions without a central authority, and it's the core technology behind most cryptocurrencies.

Crypto Wallets: What They Are and How They Work

To invest in or use cryptocurrency, you'll need a crypto wallet, which stores the private keys (essentially your password) required to access your cryptocurrency. Wallets come in two main types: **hot wallets** and **cold wallets**.

1. **Hot Wallets**: Connected to the internet, hot wallets are convenient for transactions. They include web-based, mobile, and desktop wallets, such as Coinbase Wallet or MetaMask. However, they are more vulnerable to hacks compared to offline options.

2. **Cold Wallets**: These are offline storage options, such as hardware wallets (e.g., Ledger, Trezor) and paper wallets. While less convenient for frequent transactions, cold wallets offer the highest security for long-term storage of larger amounts.

Each wallet has a unique "address" to receive funds and a private key that grants access to the funds. Protecting your private keys is essential, as losing them means losing access to your cryptocurrency permanently.

4.2 Investing in Cryptocurrencies: Risks, Rewards, and Popular Platforms

Cryptocurrencies are often characterized by extreme volatility, which can offer opportunities for substantial gains but also risks of significant losses. Investing in cryptocurrencies requires an understanding of these dynamics and access to reputable platforms.

Risks and Rewards of Cryptocurrency Investing

- **Rewards:**
    - **High Potential Returns**: Cryptocurrencies have delivered impressive returns for early investors. For instance, Bitcoin's value surged from mere cents to tens of thousands of dollars over the years.
    - **Portfolio Diversification**: Cryptocurrency can serve as an alternative asset class in a diversified portfolio, potentially offering returns uncorrelated with traditional markets.
    - **Innovation Potential**: Blockchain applications beyond currency, like smart contracts and decentralized finance (DeFi), offer long-term growth potential.
- **Risks:**

- **Volatility**: Cryptocurrency prices can fluctuate wildly, sometimes within minutes. This volatility can lead to rapid gains but also steep losses.

- **Regulatory Uncertainty**: The evolving regulatory environment around cryptocurrencies could impact their value and accessibility.

- **Security Risks**: Hacks and scams are prevalent in the crypto space, especially on lesser-known exchanges or with phishing schemes targeting inexperienced users.

It's essential to approach cryptocurrency with a well-thought-out strategy and only invest what you can afford to lose. Diversifying within the crypto space by investing in multiple coins can also help spread risk.

Popular Cryptocurrency Investment Platforms

Numerous platforms facilitate cryptocurrency investments, each offering unique features:

1. **Coinbase**: One of the most user-friendly and regulated exchanges in the United States, Coinbase is ideal for beginners. It provides access to many major cryptocurrencies and includes a built-in wallet.

2. **Binance**: Known for its low fees and broad selection of cryptocurrencies, Binance is popular among experienced investors. It offers advanced trading options and a range of crypto assets.

3. **Kraken**: Known for its strong security and regulatory compliance, Kraken offers a mix of simplicity for beginners and advanced features for seasoned traders.

4. **Gemini**: A regulated exchange with a user-friendly interface, Gemini provides a secure way to trade and store cryptocurrency. It's particularly popular with institutional investors.

Key Tips for Beginners in Crypto Investing

- **Start Small**: Begin with a modest investment while you get familiar with the crypto market and trading dynamics.

- **Use Stop-Losses**: For assets as volatile as crypto, stop-loss orders can help manage losses by automatically selling assets when they hit a certain price.

- **Stay Informed**: Cryptocurrency markets are highly responsive to news, regulatory changes, and social media trends. Regularly monitoring news and updates can help you make informed decisions.

4.3 NFTs and Other Blockchain Assets as Wealth-Building Tools

What Are NFTs?

NFTs, or non-fungible tokens, represent unique assets stored on a blockchain, often used for digital art, collectibles, virtual real estate, and more. Unlike cryptocurrencies like Bitcoin or Ethereum, which are "fungible" (interchangeable for the same value), NFTs are one-of-a-kind. Each NFT has a unique digital signature, making it ideal for proving ownership of digital assets.

How NFTs Work

NFTs are created using blockchain technology, primarily on the Ethereum network. Here's a simplified breakdown:

1. **Minting**: Creating an NFT involves minting it on a blockchain, establishing a record of ownership.

2. **Smart Contracts**: NFTs are often created through smart contracts, which automatically execute transactions and enforce terms on the blockchain.

3. **Ownership and Transferability**: Once an NFT is purchased, ownership is recorded on the blockchain, and it can be transferred to others.

NFTs have become highly sought after in the art and entertainment industries, allowing creators to monetize digital assets in new ways.

Pros and Cons of NFTs as Investments

- **Pros**:
    - **Digital Ownership**: NFTs offer verifiable ownership of digital assets, which can hold significant value, especially for rare or popular items.
    - **Creator Revenue**: NFTs have built-in royalties that reward creators each time the asset is resold, making it a sustainable way for artists to generate income.
    - **New Market Opportunities**: NFTs are relatively new, with unique markets like virtual real estate and digital collectibles still emerging, offering high potential for early adopters.

- **Cons**:
    - **High Volatility**: Like cryptocurrencies, NFT values can be highly speculative, with prices rising and falling based on trends and hype.

- **Environmental Impact**: The blockchain technology underlying NFTs, particularly on networks like Ethereum, requires substantial energy, which has raised concerns about environmental sustainability.
- **Liquidity Risks**: Selling an NFT can take time, as finding a buyer for a unique asset can be challenging.

Other Blockchain-Based Assets

Beyond NFTs and cryptocurrencies, other blockchain-based assets are emerging as wealth-building tools:

- **DeFi (Decentralized Finance)**: DeFi platforms use blockchain to recreate traditional financial services like lending, borrowing, and earning interest without intermediaries. DeFi can provide opportunities for passive income but also comes with high risks.

- **Tokenized Real Estate**: Blockchain technology allows real estate assets to be "tokenized," enabling fractional ownership and making real estate investment more accessible.

Strategies for Investing in Blockchain Assets

1. **Research**: Blockchain assets are still developing. Understanding each type of asset's function, use case, and potential value is crucial.

2. **Diversify**: As with any investment, diversifying your portfolio across different asset types and platforms can help mitigate risk.

3. **Stay Informed**: Keep up with changes in technology and market trends, as blockchain-based investments evolve rapidly.

Key Takeaways

- Blockchain technology underpins cryptocurrencies, NFTs, and other assets, offering secure, decentralized financial opportunities.

- Cryptocurrency investing can be rewarding but requires caution due to its volatility and evolving regulatory landscape.

- NFTs and blockchain assets open new ways to own and invest in digital assets, with both potential and risk, especially in emerging markets.

This chapter provides foundational knowledge for navigating the world of cryptocurrency and blockchain-based assets. Whether for active trading or long-term investment, understanding these tools is essential to harnessing the digital age's wealth-building potential.

Part 3: Digital Investment Essentials

Chapter 5: Automating Wealth: AI and Financial Automation Tools

As technology advances, artificial intelligence (AI) and automation have transformed how we manage our money. Today's tools can help investors grow wealth with less time and effort, from robo-advisors and automated investing platforms to AI-driven savings apps and digital financial advisors. While these tools offer convenience and efficiency, it's essential to understand how they work, their benefits, and the potential pitfalls. This chapter dives into the power of financial automation and how you can use it to complement your wealth-building journey.

5.1 The Power of Robo-Advisors and Automated Investing

What Are Robo-Advisors?

Robo-advisors are digital platforms that provide automated financial planning services. These platforms use algorithms to manage investment portfolios based on a client's risk tolerance, financial goals, and investment horizon. After an initial assessment, robo-advisors build a diversified portfolio and handle all aspects of portfolio management, including periodic rebalancing and tax optimization. They offer a hands-off approach to investing, making them ideal for beginners or those with limited time.

Key Benefits of Robo-Advisors

- **Low Fees**: Robo-advisors generally charge lower fees than traditional financial advisors, as they rely on algorithms rather than human management. Many have annual fees between 0.25% to 0.50%, making them an affordable option for investors on a budget.

- **Accessibility**: Many robo-advisors have low or no minimum balance requirements, allowing more people to start investing with smaller amounts.

- **Diversification and Rebalancing**: Robo-advisors automatically diversify investments across asset classes (stocks, bonds, etc.), reducing risk. They also rebalance portfolios periodically to maintain the intended asset allocation, which is critical for managing risk and optimizing returns.

Popular Robo-Advisor Platforms

Some well-known robo-advisor platforms include:

- **Betterment**: Known for its goal-based investment approach and user-friendly interface, Betterment offers customizable portfolios, tax-saving strategies, and retirement planning.

- **Wealthfront**: With low fees, tax-loss harvesting, and a focus on cash management, Wealthfront provides a comprehensive solution for tech-savvy investors.

- **Ellevest**: Designed with women in mind, Ellevest offers personalized financial advice that accounts for gender-specific salary growth and career breaks.

Are Robo-Advisors Right for You?

While robo-advisors are suitable for investors looking for an affordable, low-maintenance way to grow wealth, they may not be ideal for those with more complex financial needs or who prefer more control over their portfolios. Additionally, some investors may miss the personalized insights a human advisor could provide, especially in volatile markets.

5.2 AI-Driven Savings Apps and Digital Financial Advisors

With the rise of AI, financial apps are becoming smarter and more intuitive, helping people save and manage money more efficiently. AI-driven savings apps and digital financial advisors can simplify financial planning, optimize savings, and reduce the guesswork involved in managing money.

AI-Driven Savings Apps

AI-driven savings apps analyze user spending patterns and automate savings in small, manageable increments. These apps often link to bank accounts and automatically transfer a portion of your money to a savings account, aiming to save without impacting your lifestyle. Here are a few popular options:

- **Digit**: Digit calculates what you can afford to save based on your spending habits and income patterns, transferring small amounts to savings automatically. It also offers goal-based saving for things like vacations, emergencies, or major purchases.

- **Qapital**: Qapital lets users set savings goals and create "rules" that trigger savings. For instance, you could set a rule to save $1 every time you buy coffee or round up purchases to the nearest dollar, with the extra amount going into savings.

- **Chime**: Chime offers an automatic savings feature that rounds up each purchase to the nearest dollar and transfers the difference into a savings account, making saving effortless.

Digital Financial Advisors

Digital financial advisors, also called "hybrid" advisors, combine AI technology with access to human advisors. These platforms offer more than just automated investment management; they also provide personalized advice from financial professionals when needed. Hybrid advisors can be helpful for those who prefer a degree of human interaction but want to benefit from lower fees than traditional financial advisors.

- **Vanguard Personal Advisor Services**: This service pairs users with a dedicated human advisor who provides advice, while Vanguard's algorithms handle investment management and rebalancing.

- **Schwab Intelligent Portfolios Premium**: Schwab offers automated investment portfolios combined with unlimited access to human advisors for a low monthly fee, making it an affordable option for those who want ongoing advice.

- **Personal Capital**: While primarily a financial planning app, Personal Capital offers access to human advisors and tools that allow users to track spending, net worth, and investments in one place.

Pros and Cons of AI-Driven Financial Apps

- **Pros**:

- **Efficiency and Convenience**: Automation makes saving easy, even for people who struggle with traditional budgeting.
- **Behavior-Based Savings**: AI-driven apps encourage saving by adjusting to your spending habits, making saving feel less like a chore.
- **Budgeting Assistance**: Many of these apps come with budgeting tools, helping you understand and manage your finances more holistically.

- **Cons**:
  - **Fees**: Some apps, like Digit, charge monthly fees. For people with smaller savings, these fees could add up over time.
  - **Data Privacy**: Financial apps require access to bank accounts, which raises privacy concerns for some users.
  - **Limited Flexibility**: Automated savings may not account for unexpected expenses or financial needs, so it's essential to regularly review and adjust your settings.

5.3 Balancing Automation with Personalized Financial Management

Automating certain aspects of wealth-building can save time and improve financial outcomes, but it's crucial to find a balance. Over-reliance on automation may result in a passive approach to personal finance, where important decisions are overlooked. Understanding where and how to use these tools to your advantage is key to achieving financial security.

Automation Complements, Not Replaces, Personal Oversight

Even with advanced automation, certain aspects of financial management require a personal touch. Regularly reviewing financial goals, assessing risk tolerance, and adapting to changes in income or expenses are essential parts of wealth management that shouldn't be left solely to AI.

- **Set and Review Goals**: Automated tools can help reach goals like retirement savings, but it's up to you to set those goals in the first place. Periodically reviewing and adjusting your financial goals can ensure that your automated plan aligns with your changing priorities.

- **Evaluate Investment Performance**: While robo-advisors and digital financial advisors can manage your investments, regularly checking your portfolio's performance and understanding why certain assets are included can lead to a more informed investment strategy.

- **Risk Management**: Many automation tools offer risk-adjusted portfolios, but it's essential to adjust your risk tolerance as life circumstances change. Job changes, family growth, or upcoming expenses might require a different approach to managing risk.

Mixing Automated and Manual Approaches

For an effective strategy, consider using automation for tasks like savings and basic investing, while keeping manual control over areas requiring more judgment, such as large investment decisions or high-stakes budgeting.

1. **Automatic Savings, Manual Spending Adjustments**: Let AI-driven apps automate small savings, but manually adjust your budget to accommodate any significant changes in your income or expenses.

2. **Automated Investing, Regular Reviews**: Use robo-advisors for ease of investing but review your portfolio's performance periodically to stay informed and make adjustments if needed.

3. **Balancing AI with Human Expertise**: Hybrid advisors or consulting with a human advisor for complex financial matters can offer the best of both worlds, blending automation's efficiency with human insight.

The Role of Education and Awareness

Automation is a powerful tool, but education is the ultimate safeguard for building and preserving wealth. Understanding how each tool functions, its potential impact on your finances, and where manual intervention might be necessary empowers you to make more informed decisions. Educating yourself on financial literacy topics—such as budgeting, investing principles, and tax implications—will enable you to leverage automation while staying in control of your wealth-building journey.

Key Takeaways

- **AI-powered tools like robo-advisors and digital financial advisors simplify investing and managing money, making it accessible and affordable for more people.**

- **Automated savings apps use behavioral insights to help users save effortlessly, but fees and data privacy remain considerations.**

- **Balancing automation with personal oversight ensures that your financial strategy remains adaptive to changing circumstances and aligned with your long-term goals.**

Financial automation can provide convenience and increase the efficiency of wealth-building, but it's essential to stay informed and involved in key financial decisions. By leveraging the power of AI and automation while maintaining control over your financial direction, you can enhance your wealth-building strategy in the digital age.

Part 3: Digital Investment Essentials

Chapter 6: Navigating the Fintech World: Apps and Platforms for Financial Growth

The rapid evolution of fintech has transformed the landscape of personal finance. Today, a variety of apps and platforms enable individuals to manage, invest, and grow their wealth with ease. This chapter will guide you through some of the most popular fintech tools for investment, budgeting, and saving, explore alternative financial models like peer-to-peer lending and crowdfunding, and help you choose the fintech solutions that best align with your financial goals.

6.1 Overview of Top Fintech Tools for Investment, Budgeting, and Saving

Fintech, short for financial technology, encompasses a broad range of applications designed to simplify and enhance financial management. These tools are reshaping how people handle their money by providing new ways to invest, save, and budget. Whether you're a seasoned investor or just starting, these apps and platforms can streamline your financial journey.

Investment Apps

Investment apps have made stock trading, ETF investments, and even real estate investments accessible to a wide audience. Many of these apps offer low fees, user-friendly interfaces, and educational resources for beginner investors.

- **Robinhood**: Known for its commission-free trading, Robinhood allows users to invest in stocks, ETFs, and cryptocurrencies with no minimum balance. It's an ideal platform for beginners who want to get a feel for the market.

- **Acorns**: Acorns rounds up your everyday purchases to the nearest dollar and invests the spare change into a diversified portfolio. This app is designed for hands-off investing, making it great for users who want to grow their money without active trading.

- **Wealthfront**: A robo-advisor that automates investing based on your risk profile and financial goals. Wealthfront also offers features like tax-loss harvesting and financial planning tools.

Budgeting and Saving Apps

Budgeting apps help users track their income, expenses, and savings goals. Some also offer features like bill reminders and credit score monitoring, making them comprehensive tools for financial health.

- **Mint**: Mint is one of the most popular budgeting apps, offering tools to track spending, categorize expenses, and create a monthly budget. The app syncs with your bank accounts to provide a real-time view of your finances.

- **You Need a Budget (YNAB)**: Known for its proactive budgeting approach, YNAB encourages users to give every dollar a job. It's designed to help people break the paycheck-to-paycheck cycle by prioritizing spending based on their goals.

- **Digit**: This app automates savings by analyzing your spending patterns and transferring small amounts into savings. Digit is great for individuals who want to save without actively budgeting every expense.

High-Yield Savings and Cash Management Apps

Several fintech platforms also offer cash management accounts with higher interest rates than traditional savings accounts. These accounts often come with benefits like no fees, easy transfers, and tools to help grow your savings.

- **Chime**: Chime offers a high-yield savings account, with the added benefit of automatic saving tools like round-up transfers and paycheck direct deposits.

- **Ally Bank**: As an online bank, Ally provides competitive interest rates on savings accounts and CDs. Its user-friendly app makes it easy to manage savings and track interest growth.

- **Marcus by Goldman Sachs**: Known for its high-yield savings accounts and personal loan offerings, Marcus combines the trustworthiness of a traditional bank with the convenience of fintech.

6.2 Peer-to-Peer Lending, Crowdfunding, and Micro-Investing

The fintech world isn't just limited to traditional investments and savings tools. New platforms in peer-to-peer lending, crowdfunding, and micro-investing are opening up alternative pathways for financial growth.

Peer-to-Peer (P2P) Lending

Peer-to-peer lending platforms allow individuals to lend money directly to other individuals or small businesses, bypassing traditional banks. This setup provides potentially higher returns for lenders and accessible funding for borrowers, albeit with increased risk.

- **Prosper**: Prosper is one of the oldest P2P lending platforms in the U.S., where investors can fund personal loans with varying levels of risk and return.

- **LendingClub**: LendingClub offers a range of loan options, including personal loans and small business financing. Investors can choose loans based on risk level and expected returns.

Advantages and Risks of P2P Lending

While P2P lending offers attractive returns, it also carries risks. Borrowers may default, and the loans are often unsecured, meaning they aren't backed by collateral. However, for investors willing to take on more risk, P2P lending can be a lucrative option.

Crowdfunding

Crowdfunding allows individuals to invest small amounts in startup businesses or creative projects in exchange for a stake or future reward. Platforms like **Kickstarter** and **Indiegogo** popularized this concept, allowing people to support ideas they believe in.

- **Equity Crowdfunding**: For investors interested in owning a piece of a startup, platforms like **SeedInvest** and **WeFunder** offer equity crowdfunding opportunities.

- **Real Estate Crowdfunding**: Real estate platforms like **Fundrise** allow investors to pool funds for residential or commercial real estate projects, with returns distributed based on the project's success.

Micro-Investing

Micro-investing apps enable users to invest small amounts, sometimes as low as a dollar, into diversified portfolios. These platforms make investing accessible to those with limited funds or those wanting to try investing on a small scale.

- **Stash**: Stash allows users to invest in fractional shares of companies and ETFs with as little as $5. It also provides financial education resources to help users build investment knowledge.

- **Public**: Public combines social media with investing, allowing users to follow other investors, share insights, and build a portfolio with fractional shares.

Micro-investing helps break down the barriers to entry for first-time investors, allowing them to start building wealth even with limited funds.

6.3 Choosing the Best Fintech Solutions for Your Financial Goals

With so many fintech tools available, choosing the right ones for your financial objectives can be overwhelming. When evaluating a platform, consider your goals, risk tolerance, and personal preferences.

Define Your Financial Goals

Start by identifying your financial goals. Are you focused on building an emergency fund, investing for retirement, or diversifying income? Here's how different fintech solutions align with common goals:

- **Building Savings**: High-yield savings apps like Chime or Ally Bank are ideal for saving an emergency fund or short-term goals.

- **Investment Growth**: Robo-advisors like Wealthfront or micro-investing apps like Stash can help you grow your wealth in a diversified, low-cost portfolio.

- **Alternative Income Streams**: For those looking to diversify income, consider exploring P2P lending or real estate crowdfunding as potential options.

Assess Fees and Hidden Costs

While many fintech platforms boast low fees, it's important to be aware of all associated costs. Some apps charge subscription fees, transaction fees, or account maintenance fees, which can add up over time.

- **Low-Fee Options**: Mint, Acorns, and Robinhood offer free or minimal-cost services, making them great for budget-conscious users.

- **Watch for Subscription Fees**: Apps like YNAB and Digit charge monthly fees, so ensure that the benefits justify the costs for your budget.

Consider User Experience and Accessibility

Ease of use is crucial in fintech, especially for users new to digital finance. Look for apps with intuitive interfaces, responsive customer support, and resources that guide you through the platform's features.

- **Beginner-Friendly**: Mint and Acorns offer straightforward interfaces and easy onboarding for beginners.
- **Customization Options**: Platforms like Stash or Wealthfront provide more advanced features and customization for experienced users.

Factor in Security and Privacy

When dealing with financial platforms, security should be a top priority. Ensure the platform uses encryption and two-factor authentication to protect your data. Look for apps with strong reputations and solid security measures.

- **Established Fintech Apps**: Mint, Betterment, and Ally Bank are well-known for their security protocols.
- **Be Cautious with Newer Platforms**: While newer apps may offer exciting features, do some research to ensure they prioritize user privacy and security.

Test the Platform with Small Investments

If you're unsure which fintech app suits you best, start by investing or saving a small amount. Many platforms allow you to start with as little as $1, so you can test their functionality and see if they meet your needs without a significant commitment.

Key Takeaways

- **Fintech platforms offer a diverse range of options for budgeting, investing, and saving, each suited to different financial goals and risk profiles.**

- **Peer-to-peer lending, crowdfunding, and micro-investing provide alternative pathways to traditional finance, allowing you to diversify income and explore new investment opportunities.**

- **Choosing the right fintech solution depends on your goals, budget, experience level, and willingness to explore both mainstream and alternative financial models.**

Navigating the fintech world may seem complex, but with a clear understanding of your goals and an awareness of available tools, you can harness digital finance to enhance your financial growth and control.

Part 4: Leveraging Knowledge and Skills for Wealth

Chapter 7: Upskilling for Profit: The Power of Online Education

The rise of digital tools and global access to education has transformed the way people learn, enabling individuals to upskill and boost their earning potential like never before. Upskilling—learning new skills to stay relevant or advance in your field—can help you negotiate higher pay, diversify your income streams, or even start your own business. This chapter explores high-demand skills, the best platforms for online learning and certification, and strategies for applying your skills to achieve financial growth.

7.1 High-Demand Skills in the Tech and Digital Space

As technology reshapes industries, the demand for tech and digital skills continues to surge. Acquiring expertise in these areas can open doors to lucrative career paths, remote work opportunities, and entrepreneurial ventures. Here are some high-demand skills that offer significant earning potential:

1. Data Analysis and Data Science

Data is now regarded as one of the most valuable resources in the digital age, with data analysts and scientists playing a critical role in interpreting and leveraging information to make informed decisions. Skills in programming languages like Python, R, and SQL are essential for this field, along with familiarity with data visualization tools like Tableau or Power BI. Many companies value these skills highly, given the insights they bring to business strategies and market trends.

2. Digital Marketing

Digital marketing encompasses a range of skills, including content marketing, social media management, SEO, email marketing, and pay-per-click advertising. As more businesses shift to online platforms, digital marketing professionals are increasingly sought after to help companies reach and engage their target audiences. Upskilling in digital marketing can lead to roles such as digital strategist, content manager, or social media consultant, and is also ideal for anyone interested in launching their own online brand.

3. Software Development

Software developers are in constant demand as companies continue to innovate and digitize. Skills in coding languages like JavaScript, Python, C++, and frameworks such as React or Django are highly valuable. With these skills, you could pursue a career in web development, mobile app development, or backend engineering, all of which offer strong earning potential and remote work flexibility.

4. Cybersecurity

As digital security becomes a top concern for businesses and individuals, cybersecurity experts play a vital role in protecting data and systems from cyber threats. Certifications such as Certified Information Systems Security Professional (CISSP) or CompTIA Security+ can be pathways to high-paying roles in cybersecurity. Cybersecurity skills are especially valuable as companies face increasing cyber threats and need skilled professionals to safeguard their digital assets.

5. UX/UI Design

User Experience (UX) and User Interface (UI) design are central to creating accessible and appealing digital products. UX/UI designers are responsible for crafting intuitive, user-friendly websites and apps, and their work is crucial in driving user engagement. A strong portfolio, knowledge of design tools like Adobe XD or Figma, and an understanding of user psychology can make this a lucrative field, whether you pursue a career in a company or offer freelance design services.

6. Project Management

With the rise of complex digital projects, project managers are essential for keeping teams on track, meeting deadlines, and ensuring that projects meet quality standards. Skills in agile methodologies, tools like Asana, Jira, or Trello, and certifications such as Project Management Professional (PMP) are in high demand, especially as companies adopt remote work structures.

7.2 Best Platforms for Online Learning and Certification

Thanks to the proliferation of online learning platforms, upskilling has never been easier or more accessible. Here are some of the best platforms for acquiring new skills, earning certifications, and positioning yourself for career growth:

1. Coursera

Coursera partners with top universities and organizations worldwide, offering a wide array of courses in data science, programming, digital marketing, and more. Many courses are free to audit, and certifications or degrees are available for a fee. Coursera's "Specializations" and "Professional Certificates" are excellent for those seeking in-depth expertise in specific fields.

2. LinkedIn Learning

LinkedIn Learning offers thousands of courses across various industries, from business and tech to creative skills. Its library is continually updated to reflect emerging skills and trends, and its integration with LinkedIn can enhance your professional profile with course completion badges.

3. Udacity

Udacity is known for its "Nanodegree" programs, which focus on tech-driven skills such as AI, machine learning, web development, and data science. These programs are created with industry leaders like Google and IBM, providing job-ready training for in-demand careers. Udacity's real-world projects and mentor support are ideal for career-focused learners.

4. edX

edX offers courses from universities like Harvard, MIT, and UC Berkeley, making it a prestigious platform for online education. In addition to free courses, edX provides professional certificate programs and online master's degrees in fields like data science, business, and healthcare.

5. Skillshare

Skillshare is a popular platform for creative skills, such as graphic design, photography, and digital marketing. While it offers classes on more technical skills as well, its focus on creativity makes it a great option for freelancers and entrepreneurs looking to broaden their skill set.

6. Google Skillshop and Meta Blueprint

For those interested in digital marketing, Google Skillshop provides certifications in Google Ads, Google Analytics, and other tools in the Google ecosystem. Similarly, Meta Blueprint offers courses on advertising and managing businesses on Facebook and Instagram. Both are free and widely recognized within the marketing industry.

7.3 Using Your New Skills to Negotiate Higher Pay or Start a Side Business

Once you've gained new skills, leveraging them to increase your income is the next step. Whether you're looking to negotiate a raise, secure a promotion, or create an additional income stream, here are ways to use your skills effectively:

1. Negotiate a Higher Salary

Armed with in-demand skills, you're in a stronger position to negotiate higher pay in your current job. Approach negotiations by highlighting how your new skills benefit the company. Emphasize how your expertise can enhance project outcomes, reduce costs, or drive revenue. Consider gathering examples of how your skills have already positively impacted your work or contributed to company goals.

2. Pursue a Promotion or Career Pivot

Upskilling can also qualify you for internal promotions or lateral moves to roles with higher earning potential. For example, if you've developed skills in data analysis or project management, you may be able to move from a generalist role to a specialized, better-paying position. Use your new skills as leverage to transition into a role that aligns with your career goals.

3. Start a Freelance Career

Freelancing allows you to monetize your skills independently, giving you the flexibility to work on various projects and set your own rates. Platforms like Upwork, Fiverr, and Freelancer connect skilled professionals with clients worldwide. If you've gained expertise in fields like web development, digital marketing, or graphic design, freelancing can be an effective way to earn additional income.

- **Set Up a Profile**: Use freelance platforms to build a profile showcasing your skills, certifications, and completed projects. A well-curated profile can attract potential clients and lead to lucrative projects.
- **Build a Portfolio**: Collect examples of your work and feedback from clients to showcase your abilities. A strong portfolio is essential in securing higher-paying freelance projects.

4. Launch a Side Business

If you have a unique skill or service to offer, consider starting a side business. For instance, a digital marketing expert could offer consulting services to small businesses, or a web developer could create websites for local businesses. A side business can gradually grow into a significant income source, especially if you leverage online marketplaces or social media to promote your services.

5. Create and Sell Digital Products

If you have creative or technical skills, creating digital products like e-books, online courses, templates, or stock photography can generate passive income. Platforms like Teachable, Gumroad, and Etsy make it easy to sell digital products, allowing you to earn money while you focus on other pursuits.

Key Takeaways

- **High-demand skills in tech, digital marketing, and design offer significant income potential and career flexibility.**

- **Online learning platforms provide affordable, accessible ways to upskill and earn certifications that can strengthen your resume or portfolio.**

- **Using your new skills, you can negotiate higher pay, pursue freelance work, start a side business, or create digital products for additional income.**

Upskilling in the digital age offers endless opportunities to enhance your career and financial standing. By staying adaptable and embracing continuous learning, you'll be well-equipped to navigate the ever-evolving landscape of digital wealth-building.

Part 4: Leveraging Knowledge and Skills for Wealth

Chapter 8: Monetizing Content Creation: Social Media, Blogging, and Streaming

In the digital world, content creation has evolved from a simple hobby to a legitimate income stream, allowing individuals to make a living through their personal brands, skills, and passions. This chapter dives into how to monetize content across social media platforms, blogs, and streaming services. We'll explore strategies for building a personal brand, income-generating methods like affiliate marketing and sponsorships, and essential tips for succeeding on popular platforms like YouTube and TikTok.

8.1 Strategies for Building and Monetizing a Personal Brand

A personal brand is your unique digital footprint—the values, expertise, and personality that define how you're perceived online. Developing a solid personal brand is foundational to monetizing content, as it helps you attract and retain an audience who resonates with your message. Here are steps to build and grow a personal brand that can be monetized:

1. Define Your Niche and Target Audience

Your niche is the specific area of interest you focus on, whether it's fitness, finance, beauty, gaming, or technology. Choose a niche that aligns with your passion and expertise, as this will make it easier to create content that feels authentic and engaging. Once you identify your niche, define your target audience—who they are, what they care about, and the problems they want to solve. Understanding your audience allows you to tailor your content to their needs, establishing trust and loyalty.

2. Create Consistent, High-Quality Content

Consistency and quality are key to building a loyal following. Posting regularly, whether it's daily, weekly, or monthly, keeps your audience engaged and shows that you're committed to delivering value. High-quality content doesn't necessarily require expensive equipment but should be well-thought-out and engaging. Consider using visuals, storytelling, and humor to make your content relatable and memorable.

3. Leverage Multiple Platforms

While starting with one platform is a good idea, expanding your presence across multiple platforms can help you reach a broader audience. Many successful content creators repurpose their content for different platforms, adjusting for the unique formats and audiences of each. For example, a YouTube video could be edited into short clips for Instagram Reels or TikTok, maximizing visibility.

4. Engage with Your Audience

Building a personal brand is not just about broadcasting your message but also about engaging with your audience. Respond to comments, ask for feedback, and hold Q&A sessions to create a sense of community. The more connected your audience feels, the more likely they are to support and share your content, helping you grow organically.

8.2 Social Media Income Streams: Affiliate Marketing, Ads, and Sponsorships

Once you have a stable following, monetizing your social media presence becomes a viable opportunity. Below are three common ways to earn income through social media:

1. Affiliate Marketing

Affiliate marketing involves promoting products or services and earning a commission for every sale made through your unique referral link. This method works well on platforms like Instagram, YouTube, and blogs, where you can create content around products you genuinely recommend to your audience. Affiliate marketing requires a balance; over-promoting products can turn followers away, so it's best to endorse products that align with your brand and offer value to your audience.

To succeed in affiliate marketing:

- Choose affiliate programs relevant to your niche, such as Amazon Associates, ShareASale, or niche-specific programs.

- Create honest, helpful content around the products, like tutorials, reviews, or recommendations.

- Use tracking tools to analyze what resonates most with your audience and optimize future promotions.

2. Ads and Revenue-Sharing Programs

Many platforms offer revenue-sharing programs where content creators earn money from ads placed on their content. For instance:

- **YouTube**: YouTube's Partner Program allows creators with 1,000+ subscribers and 4,000+ watch hours to earn ad revenue on videos. YouTubers typically earn based on factors like views, engagement, and ad types.

- **TikTok Creator Fund**: TikTok offers revenue to creators with a certain number of followers and views.

- **Blog Ads**: On blogging platforms or self-hosted websites, Google AdSense and Mediavine allow bloggers to earn from ads displayed to their readers.

While ad revenue can provide a passive income stream, its consistency may vary depending on engagement and view counts.

3. Sponsorships and Brand Deals

Sponsorships are one of the most lucrative options for social media influencers and content creators. Brands may pay you to promote their products in your content, whether through dedicated posts, mentions, or product placements. These partnerships can take the form of:

- **Sponsored Posts**: Paid posts where you endorse a product or service. It's crucial to be transparent about sponsorships, as audiences value honesty.

- **Product Reviews**: Reviewing products or services aligns well with certain niches, such as tech or beauty. Brands may send you free products or pay for reviews.

- **Collaborations**: Working closely with brands to create tailored content can lead to long-term partnerships.

Building a portfolio of sponsored work and showcasing past collaborations can attract more brands to work with you.

8.3 Tips for Successful Content Creation on Platforms like YouTube and TikTok

Creating successful content involves understanding the platform's unique features, algorithms, and audience preferences. Here's how to maximize success on two of the most popular content creation platforms today:

YouTube

1. **Focus on High-Quality, Engaging Content**: While technical quality matters, engaging content is most important. Aim to provide value through educational, entertaining, or inspirational videos.

2. **Optimize Video Titles, Descriptions, and Tags**: Use relevant keywords in your title and description to help your videos rank in search results. Tags help YouTube understand your video's content, so include both broad and specific keywords.

3. **Thumbnails Matter**: Custom thumbnails significantly impact click-through rates. Use bright colors, clear images, and minimal text to make thumbnails visually appealing and informative.

4. **Leverage Playlists and End Screens**: Group related videos into playlists to keep viewers watching your content longer. End screens encourage viewers to check out other videos, subscribe, or visit your website.

TikTok

1. **Keep Videos Short and Engaging**: TikTok videos range from 15 seconds to 3 minutes, so it's crucial to capture attention quickly. Start with a hook, maintain a fast pace, and make sure your message is concise.

2. **Use Trends and Hashtags**: Participating in trends and using popular hashtags can increase visibility. However, use hashtags relevant to your content to attract the right audience.

3. **Engage with Comments and Use Calls-to-Action**: Encourage engagement by asking questions or inviting viewers to comment. Engaging with comments boosts visibility and builds community.

4. **Experiment with Different Content Types**: From tutorials to challenges, TikTok offers creative flexibility. Experiment to see what resonates with your audience, and consider using TikTok's analytics to refine your content strategy.

Monetizing Blogging and Streaming

Beyond social media, blogging and streaming are powerful platforms for earning income:

- **Blogging**: Start a blog around your expertise, using ad networks like Google AdSense, affiliate links, or sponsored content for revenue. Regular, high-quality content is essential to attract readers, and SEO practices can help improve your visibility.

- **Streaming**: Platforms like Twitch and YouTube allow users to earn through donations, subscriptions, ads, and sponsorships. Gamers, musicians, and other entertainers thrive in this space, with the potential to build highly engaged fan bases.

Key Takeaways

- **Building a personal brand** through consistent, high-quality content is essential for long-term success.

- **Affiliate marketing, ads, and sponsorships** are popular ways to generate income on social media, blogs, and streaming platforms.

- **Platform-specific strategies** (e.g., SEO for YouTube, trends for TikTok) increase visibility and engagement, helping you reach more followers and build a dedicated audience.

By effectively building and monetizing your online presence, content creation can evolve into a profitable income stream, offering flexibility, creativity, and the potential for growth. Whether it's through brand deals on Instagram, ad revenue on YouTube, or affiliate links on a blog, there are countless ways to turn content into cash in the digital age.

Part 5: Real and Virtual Assets

Chapter 9: Digital Real Estate: Crowdfunding and Virtual Property Investment

With the rise of digital finance and technology, real estate investment has taken on new dimensions beyond traditional physical properties. Today, investors can engage in real estate crowdfunding, invest in Real Estate Investment Trusts (REITs), and even acquire virtual properties in the metaverse. This chapter delves into these innovative investment methods, exploring the opportunities and risks associated with each.

9.1 Introduction to Real Estate Crowdfunding and REITs

Real Estate Crowdfunding

Real estate crowdfunding is an investment model that allows multiple investors to pool their money to fund large real estate projects, such as commercial buildings, residential developments, or industrial properties. Through online platforms like Fundrise, RealtyMogul, and CrowdStreet, investors can own fractional shares of properties without needing a substantial capital outlay. Here's how it works:

1. **Low Barrier to Entry**: Traditionally, investing in real estate requires a significant financial commitment. Crowdfunding allows investors to participate with much smaller amounts, sometimes as low as $500, depending on the platform. This makes real estate more accessible, especially for new investors.

2. **Diverse Opportunities**: Crowdfunding platforms offer a wide range of projects, from single-family homes to office buildings and warehouses. Some platforms focus on specific types, such as residential properties, while others provide access to commercial and industrial sectors. This variety allows investors to diversify their portfolios according to their risk tolerance and investment goals.

3. **Potential for High Returns**: Depending on the project and platform, real estate crowdfunding can offer attractive returns, sometimes outperforming traditional real estate investments. However, returns vary significantly, and investors should consider risks such as market volatility, property management issues, and economic downturns.

4. **Risks Involved**: Crowdfunded real estate investments are often illiquid, meaning funds are tied up for the project's duration (usually three to seven years). Additionally, since these investments are private placements, they are

not as strictly regulated as public markets, and investors could lose their entire capital if the project fails.

Real Estate Investment Trusts (REITs)

REITs are companies that own, operate, or finance income-producing real estate across various sectors, such as residential, commercial, or industrial. Investors can buy shares of a REIT through a brokerage, similar to purchasing stocks, and receive dividends based on the income generated by the properties in the REIT's portfolio.

1. **Accessibility**: REITs offer an easy way for individuals to invest in real estate without having to directly buy, manage, or finance properties. With just a few clicks, investors can gain exposure to large, diversified real estate portfolios.

2. **Liquidity and Dividends**: Publicly traded REITs can be bought and sold on major stock exchanges, making them more liquid than direct real estate investments or crowdfunding. Additionally, REITs are required to distribute at least 90% of their taxable income to shareholders, providing a reliable income stream through dividends.

3. **Variety of Types**: There are various types of REITs, including equity REITs (which own properties), mortgage REITs (which finance properties), and hybrid REITs (a combination of both). This variety allows investors to tailor their investments based on their preferences and risk tolerance.

4. **Risks and Volatility**: While REITs are less volatile than stocks, they are still sensitive to market conditions, interest rates, and economic shifts. Furthermore, because REITs rely heavily on debt financing, fluctuations in interest rates can impact their profitability.

9.2 Investing in Virtual Properties in the Metaverse

The metaverse represents a new frontier for property investment, where virtual land and properties are traded similarly to physical real estate. The metaverse consists of digital platforms where people can interact, socialize, and conduct business in a 3D virtual environment. Platforms like Decentraland, The Sandbox, and Cryptovoxels allow investors to purchase, develop, and lease virtual land parcels, creating unique investment opportunities.

1. **Buying Virtual Land**: Investors can buy parcels of virtual land using cryptocurrency, typically Ethereum, on platforms such as Decentraland or The Sandbox. Virtual land is represented by non-fungible tokens (NFTs), which verify ownership on the blockchain. Each land parcel is unique and can be customized with digital buildings, art, and even virtual businesses.

2. **Developing Virtual Properties**: Much like in the physical world, virtual land can be developed to increase its value. Investors can create digital experiences, such as entertainment venues, art galleries, or virtual offices, attracting visitors and businesses. For example, some companies host events and meetings on virtual properties, generating revenue for landowners who lease their space.

3. **Revenue Streams from Virtual Real Estate**: Virtual property owners can generate income by selling access, hosting events, or leasing their space to digital brands. For instance, a virtual property owner in The Sandbox might lease land to a fashion brand looking to showcase digital merchandise, creating a stream of passive income.

4. **Risks and Considerations**: Virtual real estate is highly speculative and volatile. The value of virtual properties depends on user interest and demand within the platform, both of which can fluctuate drastically. Moreover, unlike physical real estate, virtual properties do not have inherent utility or physical value, making them a riskier and more unpredictable investment.

9.3 Pros and Cons of Traditional vs. Digital Real Estate Investments

Investors interested in real estate have more options than ever, with traditional physical properties on one end of the spectrum and virtual properties in the metaverse on the other. Each type of investment has distinct advantages and drawbacks:

Traditional Real Estate Investments

Pros:

1. **Tangible Asset**: Physical real estate provides an asset with intrinsic value and utility, making it a stable investment option.

2. **Regular Cash Flow**: Income from rental properties is generally consistent, providing a reliable revenue stream over time.

3. **Appreciation Potential**: Historically, physical real estate has shown potential for long-term appreciation, making it an effective wealth-building tool.

4. **Tax Benefits**: Real estate investors can often deduct property-related expenses, such as mortgage interest, property taxes, and depreciation, from their taxable income.

Cons:

1. **High Entry Costs**: Acquiring physical properties requires significant capital, making it less accessible for some investors.

2. **Maintenance and Management**: Physical real estate requires ongoing maintenance, property management, and dealing with tenants, which can be time-consuming and costly.

3. **Market Dependence**: Real estate markets are sensitive to economic conditions, interest rates, and local factors, making property values susceptible to market fluctuations.

4. **Illiquidity**: Selling real estate can be a lengthy process, reducing liquidity in case of urgent financial needs.

Digital Real Estate Investments (Metaverse Properties)

Pros:

1. **Accessibility and Flexibility**: Virtual properties can often be acquired for a fraction of the cost of physical real estate, making them more accessible to a broader audience.

2. **Unique Revenue Opportunities**: Virtual properties offer innovative revenue streams through digital experiences, sponsorships, and brand partnerships, especially appealing to younger, tech-savvy investors.

3. **Potential for Rapid Appreciation**: As metaverse platforms grow, the value of virtual properties may increase quickly, providing high returns for early adopters.

4. **Creative Freedom**: Investors can create immersive, customizable experiences on virtual land, adding value and attracting visitors.

Cons:

1. **Speculative and Volatile**: Virtual real estate is highly speculative, with prices subject to sudden changes based on platform popularity and user interest.

2. **Limited Liquidity**: Although some marketplaces facilitate virtual property sales, the liquidity is lower than other digital assets like stocks or cryptocurrency.

3. **Lack of Tangible Value**: Unlike physical properties, virtual land has no intrinsic value and depends on the success of its platform for continued relevance.

4. **Uncertain Long-Term Viability**: As a nascent concept, the metaverse is still evolving, with no guarantee that specific platforms or virtual assets will retain value over time.

Key Takeaways

- **Real estate crowdfunding and REITs** offer accessible alternatives to traditional real estate investments, with crowdfunding allowing for fractional ownership and REITs providing liquidity through tradable shares.

- **Virtual real estate in the metaverse** opens a new dimension for property investment, where investors can purchase, develop, and monetize digital land, though it comes with higher risk and volatility.

- **Traditional vs. digital real estate** both have their benefits and challenges, with physical properties offering stability and tangible value, while virtual properties provide innovative income opportunities but carry speculative risks.

Whether investing in a physical apartment complex or a virtual parcel in Decentraland, understanding the unique dynamics of each investment type is key to making informed, strategic decisions.

Part 5: Real and Virtual Assets

Chapter 10: Exploring Stock Market Options Through Tech

The stock market remains one of the most popular and effective avenues for building wealth, and technology has made it more accessible than ever before. From stock trading apps to tech-driven analysis tools, investors can now trade, diversify, and manage portfolios from their smartphones. This chapter explores essential tech-enabled options in the stock market, including trading apps, ETFs, fractional shares, index funds, and powerful tools for analyzing stock performance.

10.1 Overview of Stock Trading Apps and Online Brokerages

The advent of mobile trading platforms has changed the way people invest. Gone are the days when investing in the stock market required a traditional broker or costly fees. Today, stock trading apps and online brokerages provide a user-friendly experience that allows anyone with a smartphone to start trading. Here's a look at some of the popular platforms and what they offer.

Popular Stock Trading Apps and Their Features

1. **Robinhood**: Known for pioneering commission-free trading, Robinhood allows users to trade stocks, options, ETFs, and even cryptocurrencies without incurring fees. It's popular among beginner investors due to its simple interface and low barrier to entry.

2. **Webull**: Offering commission-free trades like Robinhood, Webull also provides more in-depth analytics and research tools for users who want a more comprehensive trading experience. Webull has gained popularity among more advanced users for its technical indicators, customizable charts, and options trading.

3. **Fidelity and Charles Schwab**: These established brokerage firms have adapted to the digital age by offering robust mobile platforms with features like zero-commission trading, retirement accounts, and a wide range of investment options. Both platforms also provide access to financial advisors, making them a good option for investors who may need guidance.

4. **E*TRADE**: Another well-known brokerage, E*TRADE offers a variety of investment products, including stocks, ETFs, mutual funds, and bonds. The platform has user-friendly tools and educational resources, making it appealing to beginner and intermediate investors alike.

5. **SoFi Invest**: This platform is part of a broader suite of financial services offered by SoFi. Alongside commission-free stock trading, SoFi Invest provides access to fractional shares and offers both active and automated investment options.

Key Considerations When Choosing a Trading App

- **Fees and Commissions**: While many platforms now offer commission-free trading, it's essential to understand any other potential fees, such as those for options trades, margin trading, or account maintenance.

- **Investment Options**: Some apps offer only stocks and ETFs, while others include options, mutual funds, and even crypto trading.

- **Educational Tools**: For beginners, platforms with strong educational resources, tutorials, and demos can be highly beneficial.

- **User Experience**: Some apps prioritize a simple, streamlined experience, while others cater to advanced traders with more in-depth analysis and customization features.

10.2 Understanding ETFs, Fractional Shares, and Index Funds

As investment options evolve, Exchange-Traded Funds (ETFs), fractional shares, and index funds have become accessible to a wide range of investors. These options provide flexible, low-cost ways to diversify and grow wealth.

Exchange-Traded Funds (ETFs)

ETFs are collections of securities (like stocks, bonds, or commodities) that are traded on an exchange, similar to individual stocks. They allow investors to gain exposure to a broad range of assets or sectors without the need to buy each security individually.

1. **Diversification**: ETFs are an excellent way to achieve instant diversification. By purchasing shares in an ETF, investors can own a small portion of many different assets, spreading risk.

2. **Low Fees**: ETFs typically have lower expense ratios than mutual funds, making them an attractive option for cost-conscious investors.

3. **Liquidity**: Like individual stocks, ETFs can be traded throughout the day, providing liquidity and flexibility.

4. **Sector-Specific Options**: ETFs cover various sectors, including technology, healthcare, real estate, and emerging markets, allowing investors to target specific areas of interest.

Fractional Shares

Fractional shares allow investors to purchase a portion of a single share, which can be particularly useful for high-priced stocks such as Amazon or Tesla. This option has opened the door for smaller investors who may not be able to afford full shares.

1. **Accessibility**: Fractional shares make it possible to own expensive stocks with a minimal investment, allowing broader access to popular companies.

2. **Easier Diversification**: Fractional shares enable investors to diversify their portfolios without needing substantial capital, as they can invest smaller amounts across various stocks.

3. **Portfolio Balance**: They make it simpler for investors to achieve the desired balance in their portfolios, as they can purchase exact amounts instead of rounding to whole shares.

Index Funds

Index funds are a type of mutual fund or ETF designed to replicate the performance of a specific market index, such as the S&P 500 or the NASDAQ. These funds provide investors with broad market exposure and tend to have lower fees.

1. **Passive Management**: Since index funds simply track an index, they don't require active management, resulting in lower fees compared to actively managed funds.

2. **Broad Market Exposure**: By investing in an index fund, investors gain exposure to a broad segment of the market, reducing the risks associated with individual stocks.

3. **Consistent Returns**: Historically, index funds have delivered consistent, steady returns over the long term, making them a preferred choice for retirement accounts and long-term investments.

10.3 How to Analyze Stocks with Tech Tools for Smarter Investing

Technology has revolutionized stock analysis, providing investors with access to a variety of tools for researching and evaluating potential investments. From analyzing trends to monitoring financial health, these tools are invaluable for making informed decisions.

Fundamental Analysis Tools

Fundamental analysis evaluates a company's financial health, profitability, and long-term prospects. Platforms like Yahoo Finance, Morningstar, and TradingView offer insights into fundamental indicators such as price-to-earnings (P/E) ratios, earnings per share (EPS), revenue growth, and dividends.

1. **Financial Statements**: By reviewing a company's income statement, balance sheet, and cash flow statement, investors can assess profitability, debt levels, and overall financial health.

2. **Key Ratios**: Ratios like P/E, price-to-book (P/B), and return on equity (ROE) help investors gauge whether a stock is overvalued or undervalued compared to its peers.

3. **Company News and Analysis**: Most platforms offer news updates and analyses, providing context around earnings reports, product launches, and other significant developments.

Technical Analysis Tools

Technical analysis uses price charts and statistical indicators to predict future price movements based on historical data. Tools like MetaTrader, ThinkOrSwim, and TradingView offer features for technical analysis, such as:

1. **Price Trends and Patterns**: Line charts, candlestick charts, and bar charts illustrate stock price trends over various time frames, helping investors spot upward or downward trends.

2. **Indicators**: Indicators like the Moving Average (MA), Relative Strength Index (RSI), and Bollinger Bands help identify trends, volatility, and potential reversal points.

3. **Volume Analysis**: Monitoring trading volume provides insight into the strength of price movements, indicating investor sentiment and demand.

Portfolio Management and Rebalancing Tools

Managing a portfolio requires balancing risk, tracking performance, and periodically rebalancing to maintain the desired allocation. Apps like Personal Capital and Wealthfront offer robust portfolio management features.

1. **Performance Tracking**: These tools let investors view their portfolio's performance over time, comparing it to benchmarks to assess progress toward goals.

2. **Risk Assessment**: Some platforms calculate risk exposure, offering insights into how changes in the market might impact specific assets.

3. **Automatic Rebalancing**: Robo-advisors like Betterment and Wealthfront automatically rebalance portfolios based on target asset allocation, ensuring investors maintain their preferred risk levels.

Stock Screener Tools

Stock screeners, such as those offered by Zacks, Finviz, and Yahoo Finance, allow investors to filter stocks based on specific criteria. For example, an investor might screen for stocks with a P/E ratio under 20, a dividend yield above 3%, and strong earnings growth. Key features of stock screeners include:

1. **Customizable Filters**: Investors can set filters for financial metrics, industry sectors, and market capitalization.

2. **Alerts and Recommendations**: Many screeners allow users to set alerts for changes in stock performance and receive recommendations based on preferred criteria.

3. **Comparative Analysis**: Screeners often provide side-by-side comparisons of stocks, making it easier to evaluate multiple options.

Key Takeaways

- **Stock trading apps** have democratized access to the market, making it easier for individuals to invest without a traditional broker, but it's essential to understand each app's fees, features, and investment options.

- **ETFs, fractional shares, and index funds** provide diversified, cost-effective investment options, each with unique benefits that make them suitable for different investor profiles.

- **Analysis tools** empower investors to make smarter decisions by evaluating stocks using fundamental and technical analysis, portfolio management, and stock screening, helping them build a balanced and profitable portfolio.

Using these tech tools effectively can provide the edge needed to navigate the stock market with confidence and strategic insight.

Part 6: Protecting and Growing Your Wealth

Chapter 11: Cybersecurity for Your Digital Wealth

In an increasingly digital world, securing your online investments and assets is as important as growing them. Cybersecurity risks—from hacking and phishing to identity theft and scams—pose significant threats to digital wealth. This chapter delves into key strategies for protecting your digital assets, identifying scams, and implementing best practices for online privacy and financial security.

11.1 Securing Your Online Investments and Protecting Your Assets

Securing your online investments requires a multifaceted approach that includes choosing reliable platforms, setting up strong protection protocols, and using tools that keep your accounts safe.

1. Choosing Secure Investment Platforms

When selecting platforms for investing, choose well-established ones with strong security features:

- **Encryption**: Make sure that the platform uses end-to-end encryption to protect data.

- **Two-Factor Authentication (2FA)**: Many platforms offer 2FA, adding an additional layer of protection by requiring two forms of identification before accessing accounts.

- **Regulation and Insurance**: Check if the platform is regulated and insured, which can protect funds in cases of fraud or bankruptcy.

Reliable platforms, such as Fidelity, Vanguard, and Coinbase, provide robust security features and are regulated, minimizing the risk of losing funds to security breaches.

2. Setting Strong Passwords and Using Password Managers

Strong passwords are the first line of defense against cybercriminals. Follow these password guidelines:

- **Use a Combination of Characters**: Mix letters, numbers, and special characters.

- **Avoid Personal Information**: Don't use easily guessed information like birthdays or names.

- **Unique Passwords for Each Account**: Using the same password across platforms makes it easier for hackers to access multiple accounts if one password is compromised.

Password managers, such as LastPass or 1Password, can securely store passwords and generate complex ones for added protection. They make it easy to manage multiple accounts while enhancing security.

3. Enabling Multi-Factor Authentication (MFA)

Multi-factor authentication (MFA) is a step beyond traditional two-factor authentication. By requiring a third form of identification (such as a biometric verification like fingerprint or face recognition), MFA greatly reduces the chance of unauthorized access. Many platforms now offer MFA through mobile apps, which send a code to your phone or use biometrics to confirm your identity.

11.2 Common Scams to Watch Out For and How to Avoid Them

Scams targeting online investors and digital assets have grown more sophisticated. Knowing what to watch for and how to respond can prevent costly mistakes.

1. Phishing Scams

Phishing scams involve tricking users into providing sensitive information, like usernames, passwords, or bank details. These attacks usually come in the form of emails or messages that appear to be from legitimate sources, such as banks or financial platforms.

- **Avoid Clicking on Links**: Instead of clicking on links in emails or texts, go directly to the official website to log in.

- **Verify Sender Information**: Check email addresses and URLs carefully for signs of fake domains or misspellings.

- **Use Spam Filters**: Email services like Gmail have built-in spam filters to catch potentially harmful messages, but reviewing the sender information and content is always wise.

2. Fake Investment Schemes

Fraudsters often target online investors with "get-rich-quick" schemes or fake investment opportunities. They may promise guaranteed returns, which is usually a red flag, as no legitimate investment can guarantee profits without risk.

- **Research the Investment**: Look for reviews, news articles, or regulatory filings about the opportunity.

- **Check Regulatory Registration**: Platforms and advisors should be registered with financial authorities, like the SEC in the U.S. or FCA in the U.K.

- **Avoid High-Pressure Sales Tactics**: Scammers often create a sense of urgency to rush decisions. Take time to assess before making any commitment.

3. Identity Theft and Account Takeover

Hackers can steal personal information and use it to take over accounts. This can happen when you use weak passwords or accidentally share information on insecure sites.

- **Regularly Monitor Accounts**: Keep an eye on all financial accounts for unusual transactions.

- **Use Credit Monitoring Services**: Some services alert you to any changes in credit reports or attempts to open new accounts in your name.

4. Fake Cryptocurrency Wallets and Exchanges

Cryptocurrency investors are often targeted with fake wallets and exchanges designed to steal their digital currency. Scammers may set up a fake exchange that resembles a legitimate one to lure users into depositing funds.

- **Use Reputable Exchanges**: Stick to well-known exchanges, like Binance or Coinbase.

- **Double-Check URLs**: Only access wallets and exchanges directly from verified URLs or mobile apps.

11.3 Best Practices for Online Privacy and Financial Security

With cyber threats on the rise, protecting your privacy is essential for safeguarding your financial information.

1. Limit the Information Shared Online

Social media and online forums can unintentionally expose you to risks if you share too much personal information. Avoid posting sensitive information like your full name, birthday, or address.

- **Use Privacy Settings**: Platforms like Facebook and LinkedIn offer privacy controls to limit who can view your information.
- **Be Cautious About Sharing Financial Success**: Publicly discussing financial success or digital investments can attract unwanted attention from scammers.

2. Secure Your Devices

Device security is as important as online security when it comes to digital wealth protection.

- **Install Security Software**: Antivirus and anti-malware programs can protect your devices from malicious software and hackers.
- **Keep Software Updated**: Regular updates ensure that your devices have the latest security patches, which protect against new threats.
- **Use a VPN**: Virtual Private Networks (VPNs) encrypt your internet connection, protecting sensitive information when using public Wi-Fi.

3. Monitor Your Financial Accounts Regularly

Regularly reviewing your financial accounts and credit reports helps you catch any unauthorized transactions early.

- **Set Up Alerts**: Many financial institutions offer alert services to notify you of large transactions, suspicious activity, or login attempts.

- **Review Credit Reports Annually**: Regular checks with credit bureaus (e.g., Experian, Equifax, TransUnion) can reveal if someone has used your identity to open new accounts.

4. Backup Important Data

Backing up essential financial data helps you recover information in case of a security breach or accidental loss. Use encrypted storage devices or reputable cloud services that offer strong security features.

5. Be Skeptical of New Apps and Software

New apps can be appealing, but many are launched without strong security measures. Before downloading any financial app, read reviews, check permissions, and verify the developer's credibility.

Key Takeaways

- **Choose Secure Platforms**: Use investment platforms with strong security measures, such as encryption, multi-factor authentication, and regulated oversight.

- **Watch Out for Scams**: Scams like phishing, fake investments, and account takeovers can target digital investors, so be vigilant and verify legitimacy before committing to any transaction.

- **Prioritize Privacy and Device Security**: Protect your financial information by limiting personal details online, securing devices, and using privacy tools like VPNs.

- **Regular Monitoring**: Routinely monitor your accounts, set up alerts, and review credit reports to catch suspicious activities early.

Investing in cybersecurity may seem like an extra step, but it's essential for protecting your digital wealth. Taking proactive measures can minimize risks, allowing you to focus on growing your wealth without worrying about potential cyber threats.

Part 6: Protecting and Growing Your Wealth

Chapter 12: Future Trends and Technologies Impacting Wealth

As technology advances, it opens doors to new financial opportunities while also reshaping the landscape of wealth-building. Staying ahead of these changes can provide a competitive edge in creating, protecting, and expanding wealth. This chapter explores how emerging technologies—such as IoT, AI, and 5G—are poised to impact wealth generation, the sectors expected to flourish, and strategies for adapting to the rapid pace of innovation.

12.1 Exploring Future Tech Innovations like IoT, AI, and 5G

The Internet of Things (IoT), Artificial Intelligence (AI), and 5G are three of the most transformative technologies emerging today. Each brings unique opportunities for wealth-building across multiple sectors, with the potential to drive new investment strategies, reshape industries, and offer innovative financial tools.

1. Internet of Things (IoT)

IoT refers to the vast network of connected devices that collect and exchange data. This technology has applications in everything from smart homes to healthcare and agriculture. As IoT expands, new business models and financial opportunities are emerging:

- **Investment Opportunities in IoT Stocks and Startups**: Companies specializing in IoT infrastructure, device manufacturing, and data analytics are expected to grow as demand for connected devices increases.

- **IoT-Driven Cost Efficiency**: In sectors like agriculture and energy, IoT can improve efficiency and cut operational costs, potentially increasing profits for investors in these industries.

- **Real-Time Data for Smarter Investments**: IoT enables real-time tracking of assets, inventory, and even consumer behavior, offering valuable insights for investors and wealth managers.

2. Artificial Intelligence (AI)

AI continues to revolutionize industries, providing tools that streamline processes, improve decision-making, and open new avenues for innovation.

- **AI-Enhanced Investment Strategies**: AI-driven tools analyze market trends and manage portfolios, offering insights that can help investors make data-backed decisions. Many investment firms already use AI algorithms to optimize portfolios and reduce risks.

- **Automation in Financial Services**: Robo-advisors and chatbots powered by AI provide personalized financial advice, manage investments, and reduce management fees, making wealth management accessible to a broader audience.

- **Predictive Analysis for Industry Insights**: AI enables businesses to predict consumer trends and market shifts. This makes it possible to capitalize on growth areas like AI-driven healthcare or automated logistics, which are likely to expand as AI adoption continues.

3. 5G Connectivity

5G technology promises faster internet speeds and enhanced connectivity, which could reshape many industries and open up new investment opportunities.

- **Expansion of Smart Cities and Infrastructure**: 5G enables the development of smart cities, where connected devices improve infrastructure management, reduce energy usage, and enhance transportation systems. Investment in companies contributing to 5G infrastructure, such as network providers, could yield long-term returns.

- **Advancement in Real-Time Applications**: Enhanced connectivity benefits remote work, e-commerce, and virtual education, which can support growth in companies within these sectors.

- **Opportunities in Augmented and Virtual Reality (AR/VR)**: 5G enables more seamless AR/VR experiences, which are expected to grow in gaming, education, and even real estate, offering new areas for venture capital and direct investments.

12.2 Emerging Financial Opportunities in New Tech Sectors

The arrival of these technologies is leading to the development of new sectors and opportunities, which can present lucrative investments and wealth-building options.

1. Biotechnology and Genomics

The integration of AI, big data, and gene-editing technology has led to remarkable growth in biotechnology. Companies that specialize in gene editing, personalized medicine, and medical AI are paving the way for breakthrough medical treatments.

- **Investment in Biotech and Health Tech Stocks**: With the potential to address chronic illnesses, personalized medicine companies can provide substantial returns. Investing in ETFs focused on genomics and biotech is one way to get involved without having to pick individual stocks.

- **Emerging Markets in Health Data Privacy**: As medical data becomes digitized, startups are focusing on secure data handling and privacy, which may offer new opportunities for investors focused on cybersecurity and data privacy.

2. Renewable Energy and Clean Tech

With climate change concerns and government incentives, renewable energy is expanding rapidly, and technology plays a significant role in this growth.

- **Solar and Wind Technologies**: Investments in solar and wind companies, as well as supporting tech such as battery storage and smart grid solutions, are positioned to grow as renewable energy becomes more widespread.

- **Electric Vehicles (EVs)**: Tesla, along with other automakers, is driving the shift to electric. Companies producing EVs and EV-supporting infrastructure (like charging stations) are likely to see long-term growth.

- **Green Bonds and Impact Investing**: Green bonds and environmentally-focused ETFs let investors support sustainable projects, providing a potential for growth while contributing to climate solutions.

3. Digital Banking and Fintech

Fintech innovations, like blockchain and digital currencies, have disrupted traditional banking. Investors are finding opportunities within decentralized finance (DeFi), digital payments, and peer-to-peer lending.

- **Blockchain and Cryptocurrency**: While highly volatile, cryptocurrency and blockchain projects represent a new frontier for wealth-building. DeFi projects allow for lending, borrowing, and staking, all through decentralized, automated systems.

- **Rise of Neobanks and Digital Payment Solutions**: Neobanks (digital-only banks) and payment processors like PayPal and Square are gaining traction, especially with younger users who prefer digital banking. These services are transforming how consumers interact with money, presenting long-term growth potential for investors.

- **Crowdfunding and Peer-to-Peer Lending**: These platforms offer alternative financing to traditional bank loans. For investors, peer-to-peer lending can offer higher yields, though with increased risk.

12.3 How to Stay Updated and Prepare for Future Shifts in Wealth-Building

Keeping pace with technological advancements is crucial for identifying and leveraging wealth-building opportunities.

1. Follow Industry News and Reports

Technology news sources, such as Wired, TechCrunch, and Bloomberg Tech, are excellent for staying updated on breakthroughs and trends. Many tech-focused publications release annual reports that review the year's biggest trends, investments, and innovations.

2. Invest in Ongoing Learning

Consider taking courses on emerging technologies through platforms like Coursera, Udacity, and LinkedIn Learning. Courses on AI, blockchain, and cybersecurity can provide valuable knowledge, enabling you to better understand and capitalize on these trends.

- **Technical Certifications**: Obtaining certifications, such as a CompTIA Security+ for cybersecurity or a blockchain certification, can deepen your understanding of fields you wish to invest in.

- **Financial Courses**: Courses on tech-based investment strategies or risk assessment can also help make informed investment decisions in new sectors.

3. Attend Conferences and Networking Events

Conferences provide the opportunity to hear directly from industry leaders, explore startups, and discuss trends with like-minded individuals. Virtual and in-person events like CES, Web Summit, and SXSW bring together innovators and investors, offering insights into the future of technology.

4. Join Online Communities and Forums

Online communities on platforms like Reddit, Quora, and LinkedIn offer real-time discussions and peer insights into new trends. Subreddits dedicated to tech and finance, for example, feature active discussions on investment opportunities, crypto news, and fintech.

5. Diversify Your Investments

Diversification is essential in fast-evolving markets. By spreading investments across sectors (e.g., AI, green tech, digital banking), you reduce the risk associated with rapid shifts or downturns in any one sector.

- **Consider Tech-Focused ETFs**: ETFs that target tech sectors or future-focused companies provide a balanced approach to diversification.

- **Venture Capital for Advanced Investors**: If you're experienced in investments, venture capital allows you to support promising startups directly, though it comes with higher risk.

Key Takeaways

- **Technological Advancements**: Innovations like IoT, AI, and 5G are reshaping wealth-building strategies, offering new opportunities in digital finance, energy, and healthcare.

- **Emerging Markets**: From biotech to renewable energy, new tech-driven sectors are paving the way for profitable investments.

- **Staying Informed**: Staying updated on future trends and diversifying your portfolio is essential to adapt to the rapid pace of technological change.

Embracing emerging technologies with foresight and adaptability will empower you to build and protect wealth in an evolving digital economy.

Part 7: Building Your Tech Wealth Plan

Chapter 13: Creating Your Personalized Tech Wealth-Building Strategy

Building wealth through technology requires more than simply adopting the latest tools or investing in popular stocks—it demands a strategic, personalized approach. A successful tech wealth-building strategy integrates clear financial goals, a diversified plan, and practical habits that utilize tech tools in everyday financial management. In this chapter, we'll explore how to create a sustainable, customized strategy that aligns with your financial aspirations, risk tolerance, and lifestyle.

13.1 Setting Clear Financial Goals for Your Tech Wealth Journey

Your journey toward building wealth through technology should begin with a solid understanding of your financial goals. Having clear, actionable objectives will give you a purpose and direction, making it easier to choose the right tools, investments, and strategies.

1. Identifying Your Short-Term, Medium-Term, and Long-Term Goals

- **Short-Term Goals**: These typically span one to three years and might include saving for a large purchase, creating an emergency fund, or building up initial capital for investments. Short-term goals lay the foundation for larger financial ambitions and require a stable, low-risk approach to ensure quick accessibility.

- **Medium-Term Goals**: Spanning three to five years, medium-term goals might include saving for a down payment on a home, preparing for higher education expenses, or establishing a robust investment portfolio. These goals balance growth and stability, making moderate-risk investments suitable for potential gains.

- **Long-Term Goals**: Long-term goals generally focus on financial independence, retirement, or other goals extending beyond five years. This timeline allows for a more aggressive approach in tech-driven investments like AI-focused ETFs, high-growth tech stocks, or crypto assets, which can grow substantially over time.

2. Defining Financial Milestones

Breaking down large goals into smaller, measurable milestones makes them more achievable and enables you to track your progress. For example, if your goal is to save $50,000 for a down payment, consider setting monthly or quarterly savings milestones to stay on track.

3. Balancing Goals with Risk Tolerance

Knowing your risk tolerance—whether conservative, moderate, or aggressive—is essential to a sustainable wealth-building plan. Tech investments can be volatile, so aligning your goals with your comfort level around risk can prevent stress and impulsive decisions during market fluctuations.

13.2 Building a Sustainable Plan with Diverse Income and Investment Sources

Achieving tech-driven wealth involves creating a plan that combines multiple income streams and diversified investments, ensuring stability even when individual assets underperform. Diversification, particularly in the tech world, allows you to capitalize on different market opportunities without relying heavily on a single source.

1. Diversifying Your Income Streams

- **Active Income**: This includes traditional income from employment or freelance work, where you trade time for money. Given the rise of remote work, consider supplementing your income with freelancing or consulting in a field where your tech skills are in demand.

- **Passive Income**: Tech provides ample avenues for generating passive income through investments or digital products. Consider exploring opportunities in real estate crowdfunding, dividend-paying stocks, or selling digital assets like e-books or courses.

- **Digital Ventures**: E-commerce stores, affiliate marketing, or content creation are accessible income streams thanks to today's tech platforms. Although they often require upfront work, digital ventures can grow into sustainable revenue sources.

2. Investing Across Multiple Asset Classes

- **Equities**: Stocks, ETFs, and mutual funds remain staple assets for tech wealth-building. Diversify between sectors (e.g., healthcare, fintech, green energy) to benefit from broad growth trends.

- **Cryptocurrencies and Blockchain Assets**: While high-risk, blockchain-based assets can offer substantial rewards if managed wisely. Start with small allocations to minimize risk and increase investments gradually as you gain experience.

- **Real and Virtual Real Estate**: Invest in traditional real estate through crowdfunding platforms or real estate investment trusts (REITs), or look into virtual property in the metaverse for speculative growth.

- **Fintech Opportunities**: Platforms like peer-to-peer lending, micro-investing, and alternative financing enable you to participate in emerging financial models.

3. Building Resilience in Your Plan

Market conditions change, and tech investments can be particularly volatile. Creating an emergency fund and incorporating liquid assets into your plan can protect you against financial disruptions. A balanced, well-researched portfolio that spans diverse tech sectors can reduce the impact of any single asset's downturn.

13.3 Practical Steps for Integrating Tech Tools into Your Daily Financial Routine

Technology offers numerous resources to streamline your finances and maintain a disciplined approach to wealth-building. Utilizing these tools effectively can save you time, reduce stress, and improve decision-making.

1. Budgeting and Expense Tracking Tools

- **Digital Budgeting Apps**: Apps like YNAB (You Need a Budget) or Mint can automate expense tracking, categorize spending, and help you set monthly goals. Tracking spending digitally provides insights into your financial habits, allowing you to identify unnecessary expenses and free up more money for investments.

- **Cash Flow Management**: For freelancers or those with variable income, tools like PocketGuard offer cash flow projections that help manage irregular income, making budgeting smoother.

- **Setting Financial Reminders**: Use reminders on your smartphone or within apps to stay on top of bills, loan repayments, or contributions to investment accounts.

2. Automated Investing and Savings

- **Robo-Advisors**: Services like Betterment and Wealthfront allow you to invest hands-free by creating automated, diversified portfolios based on your risk tolerance. These platforms automatically rebalance portfolios, ensuring you maintain the right mix of assets as markets fluctuate.

- **Micro-Investing Apps**: For those new to investing, micro-investing apps like Acorns allow you to invest spare change automatically. Over time, this small habit can build into a larger portfolio with minimal effort.

- **AI-Driven Financial Advisors**: Some platforms offer digital advisors that provide personalized investment advice. Consider AI-enhanced apps that can analyze spending patterns, predict future needs, and offer insights.

3. Maximizing Digital Income Sources

- **Affiliate Marketing and Content Creation**: Tools like affiliate programs and content analytics can enhance your reach and monetization strategy. Platforms like YouTube, TikTok, and Instagram allow creators to generate income through sponsored content, affiliate links, and ad revenue.

- **E-Commerce and Dropshipping**: Shopify and WooCommerce enable you to run online stores without holding inventory. Partnering with dropshipping suppliers or print-on-demand services minimizes upfront costs, allowing you to focus on sales and marketing.

- **Digital Product Sales**: E-books, courses, and downloadable templates can become passive income streams. Platforms like Gumroad or Teachable offer robust options for creating, marketing, and selling digital products with minimal tech setup.

4. Regularly Reviewing and Adjusting Your Strategy

Wealth-building is a long-term endeavor, and adjusting your approach as you gain experience and as markets shift is essential for success.

- **Quarterly Check-Ins**: Evaluate your investments and income sources quarterly to track progress toward goals. Identify areas where you can improve returns or reduce costs.

- **Adjusting Allocations Based on Market Trends**: Use digital platforms to monitor trends in tech sectors or economic changes, and make adjustments as necessary.

- **Tracking Your Net Worth**: Apps like Personal Capital can help you monitor net worth growth over time, offering a big-picture view of your financial progress and motivating you to stay committed.

Key Takeaways

- **Define Clear Goals**: Establish specific short-term, medium-term, and long-term goals that are aligned with your risk tolerance and financial aspirations.

- **Diversify for Stability and Growth**: Create a diversified plan that combines active and passive income, as well as investments across tech-driven asset classes.

- **Utilize Tech Tools Wisely**: Incorporate budgeting, investing, and income-generating apps to make wealth-building more efficient and accessible.

- **Stay Flexible and Adaptable**: Review your financial strategy regularly to stay in tune with market changes, evolving tech, and personal goals.

Creating a tech wealth-building strategy takes discipline, but with a clear plan and the right tools, you can effectively harness technology to achieve lasting financial growth and security.

Part 7: Building Your Tech Wealth Plan

Chapter 14: Balancing Traditional and Tech-Driven Approaches to Wealth

As technology reshapes finance, combining traditional investment strategies with innovative tech-driven opportunities can offer a balanced and resilient path to wealth-building. This approach allows you to benefit from the stability of time-tested methods while seizing the growth potential of emerging tech markets. In this chapter, we'll explore how to merge these two realms, build a well-rounded portfolio, and keep a steady, long-term perspective in a rapidly changing financial landscape.

14.1 Combining Traditional Investments with Tech Opportunities

Incorporating both traditional and tech investments helps create a diversified portfolio that taps into the advantages of both stability and growth. Traditional assets provide reliable returns, while tech-driven investments have higher growth potential, especially as the digital economy expands.

1. Understanding the Benefits of Each Approach

- **Traditional Investments**: These include stocks, bonds, real estate, and mutual funds. Traditional investments are often backed by long-standing companies or physical assets, offering stability and predictable returns over time. For instance, bonds can provide steady income, while dividend stocks from established companies offer regular cash flow with low volatility.

- **Tech-Driven Investments**: Digital assets like cryptocurrencies, NFTs, and tech startups have gained popularity for their growth potential. While these investments are often more volatile, they can deliver high returns in shorter time frames. In addition, tech innovations like peer-to-peer lending, robo-advisors, and micro-investing apps allow for broader accessibility and lower entry points, appealing to new investors.

2. Allocating Between Traditional and Tech Investments

- **Balanced Allocation**: Combining both approaches can mitigate risks while allowing for exposure to tech's potential rewards. For example, if you're conservative, you might allocate 70% to traditional assets (like blue-chip stocks and bonds) and 30% to tech-driven assets. Those with a higher risk tolerance might consider a more even split, adjusting over time based on personal experience and changing market conditions.

- **Asset Diversification Across and Within Categories**: Consider diversifying within each category as well. For example, in traditional investments, hold a mix of stocks, bonds, and real estate. In tech-driven assets, look into multiple areas such as cryptocurrency, digital real estate, and high-growth tech stocks. This way, you're protected from significant losses if one type of investment underperforms.

3. Leveraging Hybrid Platforms for Both Traditional and Tech Investments

Modern investing platforms often blend traditional and tech assets. Many brokerages now offer options for trading stocks, ETFs, and cryptocurrencies, along with features like robo-advisors. This setup allows you to manage both types of investments in one place and track your progress more easily.

14.2 Creating a Well-Rounded, Resilient Portfolio

A well-rounded portfolio incorporates different assets in proportions that reflect your financial goals, risk tolerance, and time horizon. Building a resilient portfolio requires balancing liquidity, growth potential, and stability to weather market fluctuations effectively.

1. Balancing Growth and Stability

- **Growth Assets**: These include tech stocks, cryptocurrencies, and venture capital investments. While they can offer high returns, they're also more volatile. Limit your exposure based on your comfort level with risk and ensure these investments align with long-term goals rather than short-term gains.

- **Stabilizing Assets**: Bonds, dividend-paying stocks, and real estate generally offer more stability and income generation. Bonds and dividend stocks can buffer against losses during downturns and offer predictable returns, helping balance out the portfolio.

2. Incorporating Different Types of Risk Management

- **Regular Rebalancing**: Over time, some assets will appreciate more than others, which can disrupt your intended allocation. By rebalancing quarterly or annually, you can maintain your desired risk exposure and keep the portfolio aligned with your goals.

- **Using Safe-Haven Assets**: Gold, treasury bonds, and cash are examples of safe-haven assets that can add a layer of security. Even a small allocation to these assets can provide a financial cushion during downturns, allowing you to stay invested in higher-risk areas without selling at a loss.

3. Creating a Cash Flow Buffer

For investors who want consistent cash flow, adding dividend stocks, REITs, and fixed-income securities can provide a steady income stream. Additionally, holding some cash reserves ensures you have the liquidity to take advantage of new opportunities without being forced to sell assets at inopportune times.

14.3 Keeping a Long-Term Mindset in a Fast-Evolving Financial Landscape

As financial technology continues to evolve, it's easy to be drawn into short-term trends or to feel pressured by the rapid changes in markets. A long-term mindset keeps you focused on overarching goals rather than temporary fluctuations, enabling you to stay resilient in the face of market shifts.

1. Understanding and Avoiding FOMO (Fear of Missing Out)

- **Evaluating Trends Critically**: When a new tech investment (e.g., cryptocurrency or NFTs) gains popularity, it's tempting to jump in without a full understanding of its risks. To avoid being driven by FOMO, take the time to research each new opportunity thoroughly, and consider its alignment with your broader financial strategy.

- **Setting Defined Entry and Exit Points**: If you choose to invest in high-growth tech assets, consider setting predefined entry and exit points. For example, determine ahead of time when you'll take profits or cut losses. This discipline prevents emotional decision-making during market volatility.

2. Maintaining a Long-Term Perspective

- **Focusing on Your End Goals**: Regularly revisiting your financial goals can remind you of the bigger picture and prevent panic selling. Remember, long-term wealth-building is about growth over years or even decades, not days or weeks.

- **Resilience Amid Market Volatility**: The financial landscape is increasingly influenced by digital trends that can cause rapid market changes. Adopting a "set and forget" approach—investing and staying put—can help you navigate these shifts with less stress.

3. Adapting to New Financial Tools Gradually

- **Monitoring Trends Without Immediate Action**: Staying informed about fintech developments and emerging tech trends is essential, but immediate action isn't always necessary. Instead, observe how these tools evolve, gain user feedback, and assess the impact on your financial strategy.

- **Experimenting with New Tools Cautiously**: When trying out new fintech apps, digital assets, or investment platforms, start with small amounts. This lets you test the waters while protecting your primary assets, and it also gives you time to evaluate whether these innovations fit your investment style.

Key Takeaways

- **Combine Traditional and Tech Investments**: Build a portfolio that includes both traditional investments for stability and tech-driven opportunities for growth.

- **Diversify and Rebalance**: A resilient portfolio includes a variety of assets that balance risk and growth. Regular rebalancing keeps the portfolio aligned with your goals.

- **Stay Focused on the Long-Term**: Avoid getting caught up in short-term market trends. Keep your primary goals in focus and remain disciplined.

Balancing traditional and tech-driven approaches enables you to benefit from both stability and growth, creating a resilient path to wealth-building. By keeping a long-term mindset and adapting cautiously to new financial tools, you'll be prepared to navigate a dynamic financial landscape with confidence and clarity.

Appendices

Glossary of Key Terms

Blockchain: A decentralized digital ledger that records transactions across multiple computers to ensure security and transparency.

Cryptocurrency: A form of digital currency that relies on cryptographic technology for secure transactions, often decentralized and recorded on a blockchain.

Fintech (Financial Technology): Innovative technology solutions used to provide financial services, including online banking, budgeting apps, investment platforms, and digital payment systems.

Peer-to-Peer Lending: A form of lending where individuals borrow and lend money directly through online platforms, bypassing traditional financial institutions.

REIT (Real Estate Investment Trust): A company that owns, operates, or finances income-generating real estate, allowing investors to buy shares and earn dividends from property investments.

Robo-Advisor: A digital platform that provides automated, algorithm-driven financial planning services with minimal human intervention.

Side Hustle: An additional source of income outside of a full-time job, often through freelance work or entrepreneurship.

Virtual Real Estate: Digital properties or assets within virtual worlds or the metaverse, where users can buy, sell, or rent virtual spaces.

Resources and Recommended Tools

Investment Platforms

- *Robinhood*: User-friendly platform for stocks, ETFs, and cryptocurrency trading.
- *Betterment*: Robo-advisor that provides automated portfolio management.
- *Fundrise*: Real estate investment platform that offers access to private real estate investments.

Budgeting and Saving Apps

- *Mint*: Budgeting and financial planning app with expense tracking and budgeting tools.
- *You Need a Budget (YNAB)*: A budgeting app focused on financial goal-setting and tracking.

- *Acorns*: Micro-investing platform that rounds up purchases to invest in diversified portfolios.

Freelancing and Remote Work Platforms

- *Upwork*: Freelance platform for a wide range of skills from writing to programming.

- *Fiverr*: Marketplace for short-term freelance work in various creative fields.

- *LinkedIn*: Job networking platform also used for finding freelance and remote work opportunities.

E-Commerce and Digital Sales

- *Shopify*: Platform for building and managing an online store.

- *Printful*: Print-on-demand and dropshipping service integrated with e-commerce platforms.

- *Gumroad*: Digital marketplace for selling digital products, memberships, and courses.

Security and Cybersecurity Tools

- *LastPass*: Password manager to securely store and generate complex passwords.

- *ExpressVPN*: VPN for encrypted internet browsing and added online privacy.

- *Norton Security*: Comprehensive cybersecurity solution with antivirus and internet security features.

Further Reading and Suggested Courses

Books

- *"The Intelligent Investor"* by Benjamin Graham – A foundational book on value investing.

- *"The Lean Startup"* by Eric Ries – Guide for entrepreneurs to build, test, and scale their business.

- *"Cryptoassets"* by Chris Burniske and Jack Tatar – Comprehensive guide on blockchain and cryptocurrency investing.

Courses

- *"Financial Markets"* by Yale University on Coursera – Overview of financial markets, institutions, and the basics of financial decision-making.

- *"The Complete Cryptocurrency Course"* on Udemy – In-depth course on blockchain technology and crypto investments.

- *"E-Commerce Essentials"* by Shopify Academy – Free course covering e-commerce basics for building an online store.

Podcasts

- *"How I Built This"* by Guy Raz – Interviews with entrepreneurs and innovators.

- *"The Tim Ferriss Show"* – Discussions on strategies for productivity, entrepreneurship, and financial independence.

- *"We Study Billionaires"* – Investment podcast that dives into the strategies of the world's top investors.

References

The following resources provide valuable insights and research that have informed the strategies and advice shared in this book. Readers interested in deepening their understanding of tech wealth-building, financial planning, and digital investments may find these sources helpful.

Books and Publications

- Graham, Benjamin. *The Intelligent Investor*. Harper Business, 2006. – A classic guide on value investing and long-term financial strategy.

- Ries, Eric. *The Lean Startup: How Today's Entrepreneurs Use Continuous Innovation to Create Radically Successful Businesses*. Crown Business, 2011. – Framework for entrepreneurial success through iterative testing and learning.

- Burniske, Chris, and Jack Tatar. *Cryptoassets: The Innovative Investor's Guide to Bitcoin and Beyond*. McGraw-Hill, 2017. – An exploration of digital assets and the blockchain ecosystem.

Research Papers and Articles

- Nakamoto, Satoshi. "Bitcoin: A Peer-to-Peer Electronic Cash System." 2008. – The foundational white paper on Bitcoin, the first cryptocurrency, detailing blockchain technology.

- Schwab, Klaus. *The Fourth Industrial Revolution*. World Economic Forum, 2016. – Analyzes how emerging technologies are reshaping industries, including finance and wealth-building.

Web Resources

- U.S. Securities and Exchange Commission (SEC). "Crypto Assets and Investing." www.sec.gov. – Provides guidelines and insights on cryptocurrency regulations.

- National Institute of Standards and Technology (NIST). "Blockchain Basics." www.nist.gov. – A reliable overview of blockchain technology, applications, and implications for secure transactions.

- Fintech Sandbox. www.fintechsandbox.org – Offers insights into emerging financial technologies, trends, and tools in the fintech industry.

Podcasts

- *How I Built This* with Guy Raz – Stories from successful entrepreneurs and innovators in tech and finance.

- *We Study Billionaires* by The Investor's Podcast Network – Analysis of investment strategies used by the world's wealthiest individuals.

Websites and Online Learning Platforms

- Coursera and Udemy – Hosts a range of courses on digital finance, investments, and emerging technologies.

- Shopify Academy – Free resources and courses for e-commerce and digital business fundamentals.

Author's Note

This book was written to bridge the gap between traditional wealth-building strategies and the exciting opportunities emerging from digital technology. As someone who has witnessed the transformational impact of technology on finance, I've seen firsthand how individuals can leverage these tools to create sustainable wealth in the modern era. However, it's essential to remember that while technology brings unprecedented convenience and potential, it also introduces new complexities and risks.

My hope is that this book serves as both a guide and a companion on your journey to financial growth. Each chapter is crafted to provide practical insights, but wealth-building is a personal journey, and no single approach fits everyone. I encourage you to explore, adapt, and build a strategy that resonates with your financial goals and lifestyle.

Throughout this book, I've strived to keep the tone accessible and actionable. Financial growth in the digital world may feel daunting, but with the right knowledge and tools, anyone can navigate it successfully. Keep an open mind, stay informed, and, most importantly, take action. Wealth-building is not just about money; it's about achieving financial freedom and creating the life you envision.

Thank you for joining me on this journey. Let's embrace the future with confidence, curiosity, and a commitment to continuous learning.

— Oluchi Ike

www.ingramcontent.com/pod-product-compliance
Lightning Source LLC
Chambersburg PA
CBHW082109220526
45472CB00009B/2109